Dedication

To the great salespeople that I have had the privilege of working with. Thank you.

Audra (Murray) Rodriguez

Dave Anderson

Dave Grenell

David 'Gene' Acors

Jack Gschwind

Joe Dantonio

John Eiden

Justin Matos

Linda Wilson

Mary Ellen Sadzikowski

Mike Eiden

Mike Skuratovich

Ladell Wills

Pepe Luna

William 'Skip' Daly

With special thanks to Nadila Haynes and Abby Milligan for their assistance in publishing and marketing research.

Fresh Breath

is the Key to the

People Business!

Lessons from
47,000
face-to-face sales calls

Thomas J Hoffman

and

Cynthia D Hoffman

Published by Hoffman Business Consulting Press, Detroit, Michigan.

Cover by Tori VanLooy

Available on Amazon

ISBN -9 798684 113802

Table of Contents

Introduction

47,000

$3,950,000,000

500

This is my sales career in numbers. I have made face-to-face sales calls to over 47,000 people in my 30 + years in sales. My direct reports and I have sold over three billion nine hundred and fifty million dollars in goods and services and I have managed over 500 salespeople. This book contains the lessons that I have learned from personal sales calls, managing salespeople, conducting and attending sales training and teaching college sales and business classes.

After achieving success in sales and sales management I started teaching sales and decided to write this book to share the many lessons that I have learned. Another reason for writing this book is that most firms (including the ones' that I have worked for) provide little to no sales training beyond product training with features and benefits, disguised as sales training. I have learned that most sales people are hungry for the knowledge that will help them increase sales and advance in their sales careers. Most of what I have learned over the years has been through trial and error, reading, researching, networking, being a mentor and mentee, keeping my eyes open, listening, asking questions and taking risks. I have included the lessons that have helped me build a successful career in sales and they can help you do the same. I have found that learning and practicing the basics is a sure-fire way to sales success. Some of the lessons in the book may seem basic but I have seen many experienced salespeople become sloppy and lazy and forget the basics. Even the top sales professionals have sales and/or life coaches to keep them on track, just like top athletes have coaches to make sure they practice and continue to improve.

This is unlike any sales book you have ever read. Most sales books that I have read contain no research and site no sources. Is the person writing the book the ultimate expert on sales and knows everything about sales? Sadly, no. For this book, I have done extensive research, incorporate lessons learned from over 47,000 face-to-face sales calls, site over 30 sources and discuss what the real experts say about improving as a salesperson.

The title for the book came from a couple of different sources. In the 1970's sitcom *WKRP in Cincinnati*, one of the characters, Disc Jockey Venus Flytrap, said something similar about Fresh Breath and the People Business and it always stuck with me. Another source is my father who was a VP of sales for a large manufacturing company and I remember as a kid he always carried a roll of Certs breath mints in his pocket.

There are obviously many things that will determine your success in sales and a good first impression is one of them.

Chapter 1

Nothing Happens Until Somebody Sells Something

My first position in sales was with a car rental firm. I started as a manager trainee and I was promoted to branch manager after just 6 months and the next year won a national manager of the year award. I was promoted to district manager within two years, so my career was going well. I was lucky to work with some good managers and fellow employees. As a branch manager my branches sales percentage of rental car insurance, you know, the coverage that no one buys, was 81%. I quickly learned how to listen to customers and use stories to sell. I had customers in my office crying and begging me not to report that they were in an accident in our rental car for fear of increased insurance rates. Many asked to buy the insurance after the accident, but it was too late. I utilized these stories to achieve the 81% sales rate.

Everyone is a salesperson and has been their entire life. Have you ever watched a kid riding in a grocery cart going through the checkout aisle asking her parents for a candy bar? She is selling her parents on the idea that it is a good idea to buy her a candy bar, most of us did this when we were kids. I have watched in amazement as my kids worked their lemonade stand or talked to people at our garage sales. They were fearless salespeople and marketers. They had no issues enthusiastically asking people what they were looking for or talking about how much they enjoyed playing with the toys they were selling. They were talking about an emotional connection with what they were selling and showing how much fun they had with their old toys.

Arnold Schwarzenegger, Governor, Actor, Businessman and Champion Bodybuilder said, … "no matter what you do in life, selling is a part of it". Arnold was one of the best self-promoters ever, achieving successes that few have. Legendary boxer Muhammad Ali was also a brilliant self-promoter. His boasting and poetry were selling his brand. He did not care if you loved him or hated him, as long as you watched him fight. If you are married or in a committed relationship you have achieved one of the greatest acts of self-promotion. You convinced another person that they should spend the rest of their life with you.

Sales is one of the most prevalent careers in the US. According to *Selling Power* magazine the top 500 U.S. companies employ 25 million salespeople.

I have had many students and sales people tell me that they are not good at selling. I explain the fallacy of this by showing them all the times they have made big sales and not even realized it. One of the activities I use in sales training and teaching is the following assessment. If you answer yes to most of these questions, then you would most likely enjoy success in sales.

Are you a better listener than a talker?

Do you usually have a bright energetic smile on your face regardless of whether you're having a good or bad day?

Do you like people and like being around them?

Do you put people at ease?

When you listen to people do you give them the impression that you don't want to miss a word that they say?

Are you passionate about causes you believe in?

When people are excited, do you share their excitement?

Do people generally trust what you say?

Do you usually inspire others to go along with your ideas?

Are you at ease with people regardless of their race, religion or nationality?

Salespeople are the economic engine that runs our economy and are essential to our economic growth. Salespeople provide tremendous benefits to their companies including revenue production, market intelligence and strong relationships with customers as the face of their firm. Salespeople make their companies more productive, improve products and processes and become subject matter experts. This does not go unnoticed as salespeople can be handsomely compensated for their efforts.

I have enjoyed generous salaries, bonuses and sales contest awards. I have also met and worked with some fantastic people, traveled to all 48 contiguous states plus Hawaii and enjoyed walking the beaches in Jamaica, "Ya Mon", hiking the rain forests in Costa Rica, "Pura Vida", and enjoying some of the best pubs and golf in Ireland, "Goin' for a Jar?", on company paid trips. My sales career has been fulfilling and never boring. I can be negotiating a multi-million-dollar agreement one day, working at a trade show the next day and calling on customer branch locations the next day. The things I like most about sales are the variety of tasks, traveling and meeting new people and building relationships with them. Another great thing about sales is that I get immediate feedback from my customers. The feedback energizes me and allows me to change course if needed, adding to my productivity.

In sales, there are parallels to others who get immediate feedback on their performances like athletes, stage actors and stand-up comedians.

"Knowing your customer means knowing what your customer really wants. Maybe it is your product, but maybe there's something else, too: recognition, respect, reliability, concern, service, a feeling of self-importance, friendship, help – things all of us care more about as human beings than we care about malls or envelopes." [20]

Are you ready to improve your sales results? Let's get started, shall we?

Chapter 2

The Salesperson Who Talks about Nothing but Price, is a Loser

I hired a sales trainer to work with my sales staff and this is the first thing he bellowed at the beginning of the sales training, **"The salesperson who talks about nothing but price, is a loser!"** This sentence got everyone's attention and stifled the "sales veteran" that had seen it all and had all the answers yet still struggled.

If price was always the deciding factor in a purchasing decision, then wouldn't we all eat fast food when we dined out? Most times price is not the deciding factor, we want healthy food, quality service, a quiet atmosphere and a comfortable place to enjoy great food.

One of the activities I do during training and classes is have everyone get up in front of the room and discuss a really good or really bad sales experience. Unfortunately, most of them are bad experiences. After listening to good and bad sales experiences we all realize that the reason we do business with someone is not because of the price.

This is one of the really good experiences that I have had. I visited a clothing store to buy a suit. The salesperson greeted me and said, "I can tell by the way that you are dressed that I would not feel comfortable showing you anything but our best suits". Who is going to say no to that? Well, I walked out of the store with three of their nicest suits. After a couple of weeks, I noticed that the lining of one of the suits was coming undone. I took the suit back to the store and the salesperson looked at the suit and said, "we have a seamstress on site and I will have your suit repaired while you wait, in the mean-time please feel free to pick out a shirt and tie on us for your inconvenience". It was no surprise that this is where I bought all my suits.

Here is an example of both a really good and really bad sales experience. I was shopping for paint for a room in my house. I went to a local hardware store and asked the young man behind the counter where the paint was. He said it was in aisle 6 and I went to aisle 6 and discovered there were a lot of options for paint, satin, semi-gloss, flat, gloss and I was a little confused and decided I would paint another day and ended up walking out of the hardware store without making a purchase. A week or so later I walked into a different hardware store and asked where the paint was. This time the young man behind the counter walked me to the paint aisle and along the way asked me some questions. "What are you painting?", "How big is the room?", "Is it a kid's bedroom?", "Do you have brushes, rollers, a drop cloth, roller trays?". He recommended a good paint and supplies, and I walked out of the hardware store with almost $200 in paint and supplies. I wonder if the owner of the hardware store realized how much revenue this salesperson was generating, I know the owner of the first hardware store had no idea how much revenue they were missing out on.

We have all heard salespeople say, "My territory is different", "That won't work in this town", "My customers are different", in trying to explain their poor sales. Well I have heard these many times and I have proven time and again that it is just not the case. It is very difficult for someone to admit that they did not prepare enough, did not make enough sales calls, did not practice their craft as they should have, and it is much easier to blame the customers, sales territory, economy, competitors, weather and politics. I had a salesperson who convinced themselves that their downward trend in sales was because of a pending presidential election. Easier than the truth which was that they had become sloppy and lazy and did not prepare for sales calls, had poor follow up and spent too little time with their customers.

I was visiting one of my branch locations in St. Louis with our Senior Sales VP when the branch manager said a competitor was selling well below our price and that was why the branch was not meeting their sales objectives. The sales VP asked the manager to look up the phone number of the competitor and they called the competitor. They inquired about pricing and the competitor quoted a price that was higher than our price. They specifically asked about the special price and were told that that price was not available. They then called another branch of the same competitor and were told the same thing; the cheaper price was not available. The branch manager realized that the 'competitor is cheaper' excuse held no water.

Another example is when a branch manager at a location in my district was struggling to grow sales and had convinced themselves that the customers and area were the issue. The manager eventually left the company and I brought in a new manager from another state, the new manager, Alan, was not from the area and had no preconceived notions about Charleston, SC or the customers. The new manager was able to grow sales beyond anything the branch had ever seen or anyone at the branch imagined would happen. The manager that left visited several months later and asked how business was. We showed them the sales figures and they accused us of making up the numbers in the reports. They had convinced themselves that the poor sales were not because of them and wouldn't believe it when it was staring them in the face. I have witnessed these turnarounds many times in my sales career, proving what Henry Ford said, " Whether you think you can or you think you can't, you're right".

'Your price is too high' is often just an excuse to not buy because the customer is confused, does not have enough information to decide or hasn't been given a compelling reason to buy from you.

I attended a talk by the former head of communications for Harley-Davidson about why people bought Harley-Davidson motorcycles. Before he spoke he put us several pictures of motorcycles to oohs and aahs from the audience, many who were Harley owners.

Harley Davidson

He began his talk by saying "It's not about the bike. Actually, many of the motorcycles you just saw were not Harley-Davidson's". He went on to talk about the Harley-Davidson culture. They sold the culture not the bikes and Harley-Davidson motorcycles are more expensive than most of their competitors.

It's the Culture

When Harley-Davidson employees attend bike events they would seek out as many bike owners as they could, especially competitive bike owners. They would ask questions and write down the answers on note cards they carried. They asked the bike owner why they bought their bike, what they liked about it, what they didn't like about it and when they were going to buy another bike. The Harley-Davidson employees, many designers and engineers would review the cards the next week and send a personal, hand written note to the bike owners thanking them for talking to them and inviting them to visit their local Harley-Davidson dealership when they were ready to buy another motorcycle. When is the last time something like that has happened to you? What biker wouldn't want to be part of a family that treated their customers so special?

My wife and I recently went on a customer trip to Ireland with 19 of my customers. When we got back we sent them personal, hand written notes recalling the great times we had with them and their families and shared pictures. Show your customers how important they are to you.

Celebrate your customers. We bring our top customers lunch, present them with plaques and mention them in our newsletters. I created a parts skills competition for my customer's parts employees.

The winners of the online parts skill test were invited to our parts conference and competed for trips and other great prizes. All competitors were given shirts, plaques and recognized on stage at the parts conference. I also send holiday emails (4th of July, Christmas, Labor Day, etc....) to all my customers with a short message wishing them and their families a safe and happy holiday.

"However, being thoughtful doesn't have to cost much of anything. In many cases small gestures carry far more meaning than big ones. Remember a client's birthday or important family event, send a handwritten thank-you note, or leaving a congratulatory voice mail are all easy and essentially free ways to create positive emotional experiences. It is all about being creative, making it personal, and having the self-discipline to follow through." [6]

One thing that a salesperson needs to ask themselves every day is "Do my customers look forward to seeing me"? Do I discover creative ways my customers can sell more product? Do I help solve my customer's problems? Do I make my customer's job easier? Am I a source of information for my customer? My father played professional baseball and he often told me that baseball was 90% hustle and 10% guts. I believe that sales are 90% education and preparation and 10% selling. Do your homework and help your customers and success will follow.

An exercise I use in sales training and in the classroom is the envelope sale. I give two people identical envelopes and ask them to sell them to me. Selling them to me based on size, color, glue quality, material, etc. doesn't work. They could offer me a lower price, but the margins on envelopes are razor thin, so the discount would be insignificant. Eventually they get around to asking me questions about what I put in the envelope, "how many I order at a time?" and "how often I order them?". Digging deeper the questions become "would you show me the documents you put into the envelopes?", "where do you store the envelopes and would a larger envelope or one with a window work better for you?". This exercise points out that customers have many needs even for something as basic as an envelope and price is not near the top of the list.

"Thousands of salespeople are pounding the pavements today, tired, discouraged and underpaid. Why? Because they are always thinking only of what they want. They don't realize that neither you nor I want to buy anything. If we did, we would go out and buy it. But both of us are eternally interested in solving our problems. And if salespeople can show us how their services or merchandize will help solve our problems, they don't need to sell us. We'll buy. And customers like to feel that they are buying – not being sold." [4]

Chapter 3

What Successful Salespeople Do

To be successful in sales you must **know your customer**, really know your customers. The same way a successful doctor must know their patient. The doctor interviews the patient, notes their medical history, reviews their test results, does a physical exam, knows their age, habits and diet, knows which medications they are taking, etc.... A doctor needs to know this and more to make a diagnosis or recommend treatment options.

In his book *Swim with the Sharks without being Eaten Alive*, Harvey MacKay introduces us to the "MacKay 66". MacKay owns a company that makes envelopes. Most people would say there is not much difference between one envelope and another. MacKay knew he needed a way to differentiate his company from the competition, thus the Mackay 66.

The MacKay 66 is a 66-item customer questionnaire available at www.mackay.com. The questions get very detailed and even intimate. Questions are grouped into the following categories; Customer, Education, Family, Business Background, Special Interests, Lifestyle and The Customer and You. Here are examples of some of the questions:

Customer- #6. Birth date, place and hometown?

Education- #12. Military Service, Discharge Rank and attitude toward being in the Service?

Family- #15. Spouses interests?

Business Background- #32. What do you think is of greatest concern to the customer, at this time, the welfare of the company or his/her own personal welfare?

Special Interests- #37. Religion, active?

Lifestyle- #40. Medical history (current condition of health)?

The Customer and You- #62.-Is he/she very self-centered, highly ethical?

Most people don't know the answer to these questions about most of their friends. Getting the answers to all 66 questions means the salesperson had several intimate conversations with their customer and are probably good friends along with being business associates. People like to buy from people they know and like and this worked for Harvey Mackay and his company.

Another way to get to know your customers is doing homework on them. The company's web site and LinkedIn are great sources of information. Also check to see if there are any news articles on your customer's company, have they won any awards or won any big contracts? Who are their competitors, customers and partners? Does your customer have a Facebook page or You Tube videos? I have discovered mistakes and missing information on my customers websites that they did not know about.

I interviewed for a sales director's position and in my research found an article on pricing strategy written by the company's CFO. I read the article and asked the CFO some questions about it during the interview.   The other interviewers, the CEO, HR Director and Sales VP knew nothing about the article. The CFO was very impressed that I had read it and was able to ask articulate questions about it. I had my champion and I got the job offer.

I had a meeting with one of my largest customers and one of the agenda topics was a price increase that my company was implementing. This is usually not a great conversation as this customer regularly pushed back on price increases. I did some homework and looked at my customer's annual report and found out that they had just implemented a 5.3% price increase to their customers which allowed them to reach their annual revenue goals. To start the conversation about the price increase I showed them an excerpt from their annual report with the 5.3% increase without identifying their company. They were taken aback by the large price increase until I told them our price increase was only 2.1% and the 5.3% was their price increase. I got no push back from them on the price increase which was the first time they had not objected. Everyone understands that you must make a profit and that costs generally go up year after year.

Visit your customer's factories, repair facilities and warehouses. Talk to their front-line employees. Work with your customer's sales people. Cultivate a relationship with as many people in the organizations as you can. Often, one champion is all it will take to get you some additional business. Find out what your customer's company does well and what their competitors do well. Become a trusted advisor to your customers.

Professor Shoji Shiba the developer of the *"Five Step Discovery Process"* for *Breakthrough Management*, says that you need to jump into the fishbowl and swim with the fishes to really know what is going on with the fish. The same way you need to visit your customer's distribution center, warehouse, repair facility. etc.... to find out what processes, tools and programs they are using and how they work.

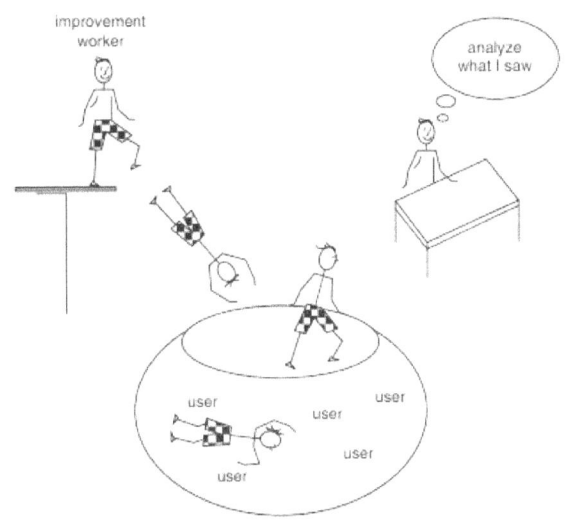

[9]

I have called on purchasing directors and managers that have worked for their companies for over 25 years who have never visited one of their own distribution or maintenance facilities. I would invite them to go into the field with me to visit their own facilities. I knew the facility employees and what they did better than most people that worked at the companies HQ.

How do successful salespeople get to know their customers? They **listen.** Here is an example demonstrating the power of listening from Dale

Carnegie's book, *How to Win Friends and Influence People*. "I met a distinguished botanist at a dinner party given by a New York book publisher. I had never talked to a botanist before, and I found him fascinating. I literally sat on the edge of my chair and listened while he spoke of exotic plants and experiments in developing new forms of plant life and indoor gardens (and even told me astonishing facts about the humble potato). I had a small indoor garden of my own – and he was good enough to tell me how to solve some of my problems.

As I said, we were at a dinner party. There must have been a dozen other guests, but I violated all the canons of courtesy, ignored everyone else, and talked for hours to the botanist.

Midnight came. I said good night to everyone and departed. The botanist then turned to our host and paid me several flattering compliments. I was 'most stimulating.' I was this and I was that, and he ended by saying I was a 'most interesting conversationalist.'

An interesting conversationalist? Why, I had said hardly anything at all. I couldn't have said anything if I had wanted to without changing the subject, for I didn't know any more about botany than I knew about the anatomy of a penguin. But I had done this: I had listened intently. I had listened because I was genuinely interested. And he felt it. Naturally that pleased him. That kind of listening is one of the highest compliments we can pay anyone." [4]

Dale went on to explain that to be an interesting person you need to be interested in other people. "People you are talking to are a hundred times more interested in themselves and their wants and problems that they are in you and your problems." [4] (Author's Note: *How to Win Friends and Influence People* is one of the best books ever written about interacting with people and we all interact with people. It is required reading for my sales teams and students)

Remember that it's not about you it's about them. I have had dozens of conversations on airplanes, shuttle buses, hotel lobbies and meetings with people where I learned about their job, family, age, college attended, reason for travel, current work projects, etc.... and I have told them almost nothing about myself. The reason is that I asked questions and listened. I used to think that I had to interject something about myself, if I asked them where they went to college I would need to tell them where I went to college. Eventually I stopped thinking I needed to do this and let the person talk about themselves. I have my sales teams and students do this exercise and

I want you to try this the next time you are sitting next to someone you do not know, ask them questions and listen and you will be amazed at how much you can learn about someone without even telling them your name. I find people are very interesting, once you get to know them, just by listening and giving them a chance to talk. There is nothing that people want to talk about more than themselves and the one-word people like hearing the most is their name.

Successful salespeople also **ask the right questions**. I have used this customer questioning grid for over 30 years with great success;

1. Decision Process	2. Decision Criteria
•How are decisions made to choose a supplier? •Who is involved in the process? •How often is the process reviewed?	•What are the most important factors in choosing a supplier? •Is service a factor? •Is quality a factor?
3. Competition	**4. Suggestions**
•Who are you currently using and why are you using them? •What differences are there among the competitors and how do they rate?	•Can you make any suggestions that would help my company to increase business at your dealership? •What would my company have to do to get some/all of your business?

This questioning grid gets you important information about your customers and how they make decisions. We refer to grid #3. Competition, as 'the truth comes out'. We would talk to customers about what was important to them in gird #2, Decision Criteria, and they would be adamant that quality and service were very important to them and were key factors in choosing a supplier. Then often when they answered the first question in grid #3 they would say "we use XYZ company because they are cheaper." You would see the expression on their face change to confusion once they realized they just contradicted themselves. One question I have asked customers is, "what does my competition do that is game changing or has a major impact on your business". I am surprised at how few customers can come up with anything. It gets the customer thinking about how little the competition really does for them.

I managed a senior sales rep who often struggled to reach his sales objective and the main reason is he asked the wrong questions. He would ask his customers if they had any problems or issues. What do you think he got in return? That's right, problems and issues. He spent most of his days working on problems and issues vs. selling. The question he should have been asking was 'how I can help you sell more products?'. Then he would find out what the customer needs to increase their sales.

In the book *The Challenger Sale*, the authors discuss how you need to be able to ask the tough questions. "Just as you can't be an effective teacher if you're not going to push your students, you can't be an effective Challenger is you're not going to push your customers. This approach is so important today with customers risk aversion as high as it is. It's funny, sales leaders often lament that core-performing reps fall into their comfort zone when selling, but arguably the bigger problem is that customers often fall into their comfort zone when it comes to buying. And that's what the Challenger rep does – she moves customers out of their comfort zone by showing them their world in a different light. The key, of course, is to do this with control, diplomacy, and empathy." [8]

A salesperson I worked with graphically explained the relationship between your comfort zone and sales success. You must to be willing to step out of your comfort zone to make the sale. Eventually you will be more comfortable in the sales zone.

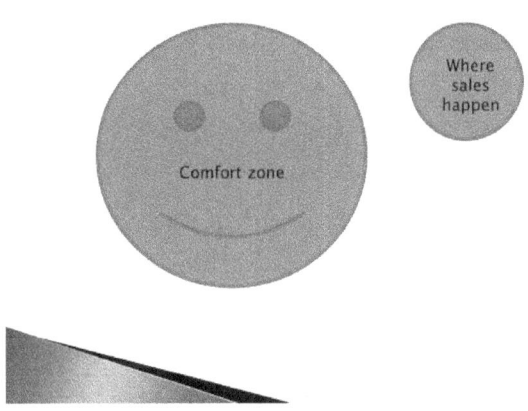

I also always make sure to "keep my head up" when calling on customers to look for non-verbal cues and items. You can often find out what is important to someone by looking at the items in their office. I have seen salespeople discussing a deal with a customer and get customer approval and lose that approval all within 30 seconds by not keeping their head up. The salesperson is talking about closing the deal and the customer is nodding their head yes. Unfortunately, the salesperson is not looking up and keeps talking until the customer starts nodding their head no. If the salesperson had kept their head up they would have known to stop talking once the customer gave a non-verbal agreement, thank the customer, seal the deal and leave.

Successful salespeople also **talk to the right people**. A young kid knocked on my door the other day and was selling popcorn to raise money for a school trip. This is what he said, "I am selling popcorn for my school trip." He mentioned the name of the school and where they were going. "Would I be able to talk to the person in your house that makes decisions about buying popcorn?" He got right to the point and asked to talk to the decision maker. I have seen professional salespeople with decades of experience that don't use sales skills as well as this young man. Yes, I bought some popcorn, how could I not.

In sales you will be shuttled to the person you sound most alike in an organization. If you have not done your homework, don't really know why you are there and don't have a clear pre-contact objective, expect to spend a lot of time with the gatekeepers and receptionists. If you know why you are there, have done your homework and have a solution to your customer's problem(s), then you may very well be sitting in front of the CEO, President or top decision maker.

In the book *Five Minutes with VITO, Making the most of your selling time with the very Important Top*

Officer, the authors draw a distinction between influencers and decision makers. "First, Influencers always want to 'see more' charts, data, recommendations, product specs, and so on from salespeople. So much so that they've earned the nickname: Seemore. Second, Influencers tend to occupy offices, labs, and conference rooms whose floors are covered, not with the plush carpet you'll find in VITO's office, but with *linoleum*."

"Something to consider: How much time are you spending in Linoleumville with Seemore?" [5]

The next time you are struggling to make a sale take a quick look down, what do you see under your feet? Are you talking to the right people?

How do you know if you are talking to the right people? You could simply ask as the young kid did when selling popcorn.

I was calling on a large account and after several meetings with the procurement director and procurement manager I knew I was talking to the wrong people. I had discovered a problem that the customer did not even know they had and had a solution that would save them over $7,195,000 a year. It was also the end of the year and if they stretched and purchased just over $100,000 more than their run rate they would get a rebate of $45,000, that's a 45% discount! The procurement director and manager did not seem interested in either one. Neither the procurement director or procurement manager were evaluated by how much money they saved on my solution and they said they were not letting year end rebates effect their purchasing decisions. But $7,195,000 in savings and a $45,000 rebate are significant savings no matter how you look at it. I knew that there was someone in the organization that would not let these opportunities pass by. I asked about the purchasing director's supervisor and other stakeholders and found out that the maintenance group was very influential in this organization. I set up a meeting with the maintenance group working my way up the decision ladder and landed a significant amount of additional business because of the savings and year-end bonus. My solution would eliminate a big pain point for the maintenance group and they were actively looking for a solution. Often the programs you sell are complicated with many moving parts. Helping the customer understand the big picture and the true value and savings can earn you loyal customers.

When I call on a company I always ask to meet the owner, President or CEO. I have met hundreds of owners this way. You would be surprised by how many people don't ask to meet them and how many owners, Presidents and CEOs are more than happy to meet people that do business with them. Once I have developed a relationship with top decision maker I keep them abreast of what I am doing and the projects and time I spend with their company. If you don't do this the company's ultimate decision maker does not even know when and how much work you are doing on behalf of their company. I am a business owner and I always appreciate the many vendors that call on me and the ones that do work on my company's behalf. It is amazing how much more credibility and respect you have with your customer's organization when they know you have a relationship with top management. You seem to get answers quicker and many things become easier.

I have found that business owners often have different objectives than their employees, even top-level employees. The business owner most often wants to profitably grow their business and is not afraid to make changes and take educated risks to make this happen. Many employees want the status quo, they do not want change or accept anything that even looks like more work for them.

I had a meeting with a customer's procurement officer and he rejected our growth plan for their business. He started off the meeting saying that he would not be able to implement any of our ideas and that business would be flat year over year. We had a meeting scheduled for the next day with several top officers and the owner of the company. We went through the same presentation and the owner said he was on board with the plan and would implement our strategy and meet our objectives. He looked around the table at the company's officers including the one we met with the day before and said, "we shouldn't have any problems meeting these objectives, should we?" They all enthusiastically nodded in agreement. The customer implemented our plan and met the objectives.

Successful sales people **know why they do what they do and can articulate it**. In his book *Start with Why*, Simon Sinek explains the why.

"WHY: Very few people or companies can clearly articulate WHY they do WHAT they do. When I say WHY, I don't mean to make money – that's a result. By WHY I mean what is your purpose, cause or belief? WHY does your company exist? WHY do you get out of bed every morning? And WHY should anyone care?" [23]

Remember it's not about you and your company's product it is about the customer and their needs.

"People do not buy WHAT you do, they buy WHY you do it." When I was selling heavy duty truck parts I sold them because I was committed to keeping my customers trucks on the road delivering the products that keep our country's economy growing. Instead of selling truck parts I am working to keep my customers profitable and keep the U.S. economy growing, that's WHY I did WHAT I did. Your WHY differentiates you from your competitors. "Companies and organizations with a clear sense of WHY never worry about it. They don't think of themselves as being like anyone else and they don't have to 'convince' anyone of their values." "When salesmen actually believe in the thing they are selling then the words that come out of their mouths are authentic." [23]

One of the best way to articulate why you do what you do is with an elevator speech. An elevator speech articulates the WHY you are calling on the customer, delivered in the time it would take you to go a few floors in an elevator. Imagine you have been calling on a company for a few months or longer and you suddenly find yourself in an elevator with the illusive President of the company, the ultimate decision maker, would you be able to articulate your why in about 60 seconds?

A good elevator speech includes the following:

Start with the goal in mind. Why are you talking?

What is the benefit for the audience? Excite your audience.

What makes you different or unique from your competitors? Be specific, as in, I can save you $ dollars, or I can improve your time to market by X days. What problem do you have a solution for and what statistics do you have to back it up?

Use an open-ended question to get the audience engaged.

Be sure you have a business card, flyer or sample to leave with the customer.

Set a date/time to share additional information.

Practice, practice, practice. Look in a mirror when you practice noting your tone, diction and body language. You should be looking at yourself in the mirror when you are talking and not looking at your notes. Be sure your elevator speech is between 30-60 seconds, less is more. Introduce yourself at the end of the speech, again it's not about you.

Here is an example of an elevator speech I have used.

Mr. Customer, I have visited over a dozen of your maintenance facilities in the last 90 days and calculated that I can conservatively save your company $20,080,000 in down time expense in the next year. A simple shift in purchasing habits is all it will take to realize these savings. I have helped 6 other customers realize similar savings. How do you currently track your down time expenses? I will be in town the next two days and be returning in three weeks and I would like to set up a meeting to go through my down time savings plan with you. When would be the best time to meet? By the way my name is Tom Hoffman and I am the account manager with XYZ company.

Successful salespeople **add value**. You can add value in several different ways.

Show you are honest and trustworthy. Sell the customer what they need.

Become a source of technical and industry information. Become a trusted advisor.

Provide training and sales and marketing support to your customer.

Be available. Answer your phone.

Follow up and regularly communicate with your customer. Keep them informed about what is going on.

Listen to your customers. Ask them what they want and how they want it and give it to them exactly that way. Ask for feedback.

Discover solutions to problems your customer doesn't even know they have.

I was discussing lost sales, for a customer, with one of my salespeople. She said that she did not know why business was down and had not asked the customer. I requested that she visit the customer and ask them directly why sales were down, there could be any number of reasons, but we wanted to know. She went to the customer's office and asked them why business was down, and the customer said there was an issue. The customer reached into a desk drawer and pulled out an agreement. She started to tell the salesperson what the issue was referencing the agreement. The salesperson realized that the agreement was a competitor's and pointed this out to the customer. The customer apologized and committed to immediately increasing purchases with us and to stop doing business with our competitor. We lost a couple of months of sales because the salesperson was afraid to ask for feedback. Don't be afraid of honest feedback as it is an opportunity to strengthen your relationship with your customer and demonstrate your commitment to their success.

I was visiting my customer's maintenance shops and it was pointed out by a technician that all their vehicles had a fluid tank that would get cloudy, so they could not see how much fluid was inside causing them to have to climb up onto the vehicle and look inside the tank for the daily inspections instead of simply looking at the tank. The tanks would also crack after a year or so and start leaking. The company directed the maintenance shops to buy replacement tanks from the supplier of the original tanks and they would all eventually have the same problems. I found an alternative tank that was made with a different type of plastic and would not get cloudy but stay clear and was guaranteed for life not to crack or leak. It was cheaper and readily available. I presented this solution to the company's procurement team along with pictures of the cloudy tank and the clear alternative tank and was awarded the business, saving the customer not only money on the replacement tanks but also inspection time and the cost and replacement labor for replacing thousands of cracked and leaking tanks every year, since our tank solution would last for the lifetime of the vehicle. The company's purchasing team did not know they had a problem.

I was visiting a favorite local restaurant with my family and a Boy Scout opened the door for us as we entered. He had a smile on his face and his troop had a table set up just outside the restaurant selling popcorn. On our way out of the restaurant we bought some popcorn. He added value by opening the door for us.

I read about a cab driver that greeted his passengers with a smile and asked them if they would like a bottle of water or soft drink. He also had several newspapers available for them to read along with snacks and asked them what type of music/news/sports they wanted to listen to during the ride. He consistently made an income of six figures as he was tipped very well. Many travelers asked for him specifically when arranging a taxi with his company. He added value by offering simple things to make travel more enjoyable.

When you add value, your customers look forward to seeing you. If a customer wants to do business with you, they won't let the details get in the way. If a customer does not want to do business with you, they will let any detail get in the way.

Successful salespeople know they must **improve every year** if they are going to sell more. In his book *People Buy You*, Jeb Blount discusses the importance of continuous improvement. "In the twenty-first century there is not time for complacency. You cannot afford the luxury of letting up for even a moment. There is not time to rest easy. Learn to take each win in stride and raise your own bar so you keep reaching higher. It is easy to look back at poor performance or a failure with 20/20 vision and find all the areas where improvement can be made. It takes self-discipline and the heart of a winner to break down a brilliant performance and then take action to make small adjustments and improvements that keep you ahead of the pack." [6]

In the book *Power Selling,* author Steve Powers says a checklist is part of your sales plan. "Create a checklist for yourself to determine exactly what you want to accomplish on the call, what information you want to garner, what questions you will not leave without asking, what requests you will make of the prospect, and what the next appointment will involve." [7]

One tool that I have used my entire sales career, to help me improve, is what I call the Sales Professional Self-Assessment. I would rate myself from excellent to poor (excellent, good, fair and poor) in the following areas;

Professional Sales Self- Assessment

Account Name:_____ Date:_____

	P	**F**	**G**	**E**
1. **Pre-Call Planning** • Preparation • Account records/update	1	2	3	4
2. Opening Statement	1	2	3	4
3. Product Knowledge	1	2	3	4
4. Competitive Knowledge	1	2	3	4
5. Selling Features/Benefits	1	2	3	4
6. Handling Questions/Objections	1	2	3	4
7. Probing Ability	1	2	3	4
8. Close – Did I ask for the business?	1	2	3	4
9. Attitude	1	2	3	4

I would also ask myself and note the answers to the following questions after each sales contact;

What was your objective on this sales contact and did you achieve it?

What was effective for me during this sales contact?

How could I have improved the sales contact?

What is your objective for the next contact with this customer?

Sometimes these questions are difficult to answer. No one wants to admit that they didn't prepare enough or did a poor job. But ask and answer them you must to improve as a sales professional. Learning from your mistakes is the best way to learn. The answers to these questions will build momentum for the next sales contact with this customer. To sell more every year you must get better every year.

"I've observed that business professionals who continually exercise their intellect are happier, more motivated, more confident, and, invariably more likable than their peers. They take advantage of every training program their company offers and are always the first people standing in line when there is an opportunity to learn something new. They invest their own money in seminars and workshops and keep their skills updated and sharp. They read constantly and are rarely caught without a book. They subscribe to weekly e-zines, trade magazines, and business publications to stay current on their industry. These professionals understand that by investing in the mind, they acquire the knowledge and skills that improve their confidence and problem-solving skills." [6]

I would recommend taking advantage of any educational opportunities that your company offers. Many companies cover tuition costs, as a company I worked for did. I was told by a colleague early in my career that I should pursue an MBA and the company had a policy of 100% tuition coverage. She told me the only thing I would regret about getting my MBA was that I did not do it sooner, and she was right.

I have cited over thirty books, articles and videos for this book and I have learned something valuable from each of them. I would recommend them all to someone who wants to improve their sales skills.

A successful salesperson **does not go it alone**. I have read too many sales books where the sole focus was on the salesperson and what they did, but, when a sale is made it is the culmination of the work of many people in many different departments both within and outside the selling company. Remember it is not about you. Successful salespeople have great relationships with their companies marketing, engineering, warehousing, pricing and other departments. They also have great relationships with their vendors and their vendor's representatives. This is not always easy as other departments do not always understand the sales process. I had one of the best salespeople that every worked with me say, "Tom, I would rather get punched in the face than to have to call my customer service team for help." Justin made a powerful statement and it indicated that there was a serious disconnect between sales and customer service. Justin's company's management was not willing to fix the problem and as a result, sales suffered, and turnover was high. This is a common complaint, especially for top salespeople who often push their support teams to perform at a higher level. It can be frustrating, but it is one of the most important relationships you will have so the time invested in improving this relationship is worth it. A 'thank you' or 'job well done' goes a long way.

Different departments within a company are measured on different metrics, but successful companies know that their goal is to sell their products profitably. Successful salespeople cultivate great relationships with those within and outside their company that support their sales. I have received many favors from my own company's departments and vendors when they were needed. You have heard the phrase, the squeaky wheel gets the oil, but the salesperson who has built and maintained great relationships with those that support their sales seem to get things done easier than those that don't.

A successful salesperson **takes personal accountability for their success**. How many times have you heard these questions or asked them yourself?

Who is supposed to take care of this?

Why is it so hard to get a simple answer?

When is this product going to launch so I can sell it?

In his book *QBQ, The Question Behind the Question*, John G. Miller points out that if you ask lousy questions you will get lousy answers and it will affect the way you think and act. "The answers are in the questions, 'which speaks to the same truth: If we ask a better question, we get a better answer. But how can we tell a good question from a bad one? What does a 'better' question sound like?

Begin with 'What' or 'How" (**not** 'Why,' 'When,' of 'Who').

Contain an 'I' (**not** 'they,' 'them,' 'we,' or 'you').

Focus on action.

"What can I do?" for example, follows the guidelines perfectly. It begins with 'What,' contains an 'I,' and focuses on action: 'What can I do?' If we ask better questions we get a better answer."

Here are some other good questions from QBQ.

"How can I support the team?'

"What can I do to make a difference?"

"How can I help out?"

"How can I provide value to you?"

"How can I achieve with the resources I already have?" [10]

Ask better questions and get better answers. The only person you control is you.

Customers are not interested in hearing you blame others inside your company or vendors for their problems, they want solutions to their problems. Blaming others paints your company in a bad light. You may think you are saving face but that is not what your customer cares about, they want someone who can get them answers without making excuses.

"When we take action, we are choosing the path of Personal Accountability. As a result, we experience the satisfaction and accomplishment – and the control over our own lives – that are so critical to success. We usually move closer to achieving our goals and those of our company. And we feel better about ourselves. It's exciting to slice through organizational inertia, to see the results that come from our achievements and to defeat Procrastination, the Friend of Failure. Action is the partner of productivity and the catalyst for achievement." [13]

Successful salespeople **network and are always looking for ways to promote their company**. I remember reading a certain business magazine every month which highlighted local businesses. I thought, why not my company? I called the editor and the next thing you know my company was part of the cover story of the magazine. How much did this cost my company? It was free PR. Press releases are another great way to get free PR (hint: including a picture can increase your chances of getting published by 50%). Press releases can include company milestones, new product launches, charity sponsorships or other interesting company information.

Many organizations are also looking for speakers for their events. This is a great opportunity to network and get your companies message out to people in your industry. I have spoken to several groups and been rewarded with referrals and new business. The groups are appreciative, and it costs nothing but your time. You can write the talk and it becomes an article that you can post on industry and business sites.

I know a business owner that requires each of her employees to join a related trade organization, in a leadership role. These organizations often have hundreds or thousands of members and a great source of leads and contacts. Being in a leadership role requires meeting attendance and involvement that goes beyond just paying membership dues. This really works for her organization and keeps her employees abreast of the latest industry trends and access to industry leaders.

I have also joined trade organizations in leadership roles and have been rewarded with a growing network, introductions and leads. Being a member of the organizations gives you credibility when dealing with its members and those that it's members refer you to.

An exercise that I do with my classes is having my students attend a networking event. Here are the instructions for the exercise;

Please write a 3-4 paragraph summary of the event you attended. Be sure to answer each of the questions below. Ideally, you are attending something related to your end career goal and you are taking this opportunity to find out more about the field, the people in it and the topics that are important to them.

Students are required to get approval from instructor of networking event before attending.

Examples of appropriate events include:

American Marketing Association
http://www.amadetroit.com/#!events/c24vq

Association for Talent Development
http://www.detroitastd.org/gdastdevents

OCC calendar for upcoming events
https://www.oaklandcc.edu/StudentLIFE/

Networking Event Write-up

Who - is the networking event that you attended? (name of event and sponsor)

What - is the purpose of their organization? (this can be found on their website)

Where - did the meeting take place? (name of business location and city)

Why - did you choose this event?

When – exact date and time…

Names of three people you met, their title, the name of the company they work for and something interesting about their job. (get business cards if you can)

Was there a speaker, if so who and discuss 2 items that they talked about?

Overall what did you learn from this experience? How will this help you with your career aspirations?

Most students have never attended a networking event before and the feedback from students is overwhelmingly positive. Many have met connections that helped them with jobs, valuable industry information or furthering their career. I asked the students to get to know at least three people at the event and find out information about their company, position, title and something interesting about their job along with getting their business card.

Successful salespeople **think creatively to solve customer's problems**. I have heard many times that the reason a company does certain things is because *that's the way it's always been done.* Successful salespeople break this cycle and think differently to solve customer problems, many of which the customer does not know they have.

One of my favorite stories that highlights creative thinking to solve a problem is the story of the flat tire. A woman is on her way to an important meeting when she gets a flat. While changing the flat she accidently kicks the 4 lug nuts down a nearby drain. She is wondering how she can get the spare on the car without lug nuts. She is pulled over next to a park and a couple of kids are watching her. One of the kids shouts to her, "I can tell you how to put the tire on your car without the lug nuts you lost".

She looks over at the them and the kid says, "take one lug nut off of each of the other three tires and that will allow you to put the tire on." Thanks, she said, that's a great idea. The kid says, "hey, I never changed a tire before, but I'm pretty good at math."

Thinking creatively or 'out of the box' is a hallmark of successful salespeople. In his book *Thinkertoys: a handbook of creative thinking techniques*, Michael Michalko lists and explains dozens of creative thinking techniques. Many of the techniques have been use by governments, the Department of Defense, the CIA, and some of the most well know companies in the world.

The technique that I have used in sales training and the classroom is called **Cra**zy Idea. Here is the problem that I pose;

You are a manager of a retail store selling consumer electronics and supervise 20 employees. The busy Holiday season is coming up and you are worried because you have a lot of absenteeism and many employees do not show up for work on time causing customer service issues. Your boss met with you today and is putting pressure on you to improve your team's performance.

Your company has been in business for 20 years and includes the owner, the director of operations, two managers including you and 40 retail associates along with accounts payable and receivable, inside phone sales staff, IT support and service staff.

What ideas can you come up with that will allow you to improve your absentee rate and get employees to show up on time?

The first step is to generate the most absurd or crazy ideas about the problem. The crazier the better. Here is a list of some of the crazy ideas.

Offer 20 minutes of nap time for every hour worked

If they have perfect attendance and are never late throughout the year give the employee $1,000,000

Give employees a 3-month vacation for perfect attendance

Kidnap the workers kids and pets and don't let them see them until after their shift

Next, we select one of the absurd ideas. Giving an employee a 3-month vacation for perfect attendance.

Next, we list the features and benefits of the absurd idea;

Employees will be well rested and happier after a long vacation

Employees will feel less stress

Employees will be able to spend more time with their families

Next, we select one of the features and extract the principle essence of the feature and build it into a practical idea.

Principle: If you make your employees happy they are going to be more likely to show up for work on time

Idea: Less stressed, happier and more productive employees

What does the idea look like? We can offer employees a bonus week of vacation during the slow season if they have perfect attendance during the busy holiday season.

We took a crazy idea and turned it into a practical, workable solution to the problem. Great salespeople are not afraid to look at customer problems differently and create novel solutions. [31]

Chapter 4

Preparing for and Executing Sales Meetings and Presentations

When you set up a sales meeting or presentation control as much of the process as you can. One way I do this is to set the agenda for the meeting. Here are two examples of an agendas I sent to one of my customers;

Agenda #1

Introductions

Current Programs

Outstanding Bids

XYZ Company Value

Purchasing Scorecard

Purchase Compliance

Product Strengths

Action Items

Agenda #2

Introductions

Think Differently

Scorecard Results

Category Trends

Spend by Location

Category Opportunities

Action Plan

I always ask the customer if there is anything they want to add to the agenda. This gives you a heads up to prepare for any items the customer wants to discuss. I also ask who will be attending the meeting and their role in the company. I then do research on each individual attending. LinkedIn is a great research tool giving you information on a person's current job and responsibilities, past positions, schools attended and if you have any professional contacts in common. I also know how much time I will have to present and can plan accordingly.

I also find out what type of room we will be meeting in, intimate conference room or large auditorium and if a projector and screen are available. I always carry an adapter that allows my laptop USB port to project through USB, VGA, CAT 5 or HDMI. It has come in handy many times. Another device I always carry is a wireless presenter with laser pointer that allows me to progress slides. I can then stand and move around the room when I am presenting. Be prepared.

A word to the wise, if you are going to have dinner with the customer have it the night before the presentation and not after. I have seen customers ask for more or nibble away at the agreed deal after they have had a cocktail or two at dinner. I have also seen deals fall apart or erode during dinners after the meeting. Dinner prior to the meeting is a good way to get acquainted and get comfortable with the customer and maybe get some insight into what they are looking for or want. Depending on what you learn this will give you time to add discussion points or focus areas before the next day's meeting. Many people are more comfortable away from the office and this gives you an opportunity to really get to know your customers with no time demands or interruptions. If you invite the customer to dinner do it with a phone call and not an email. Many customers operate under strict guidelines set down by their employer concerning gifts and awards. Dinners usually do not fall into this category, but it is still more comfortable for the customer not to have the email trail.

Another thing to keep in mind is that a meal with a client is still business.

"A luncheon meeting with a client or prospective customer is a sales call with tableware. You are there to ask questions, to listen, and to get a commitment. You are not there to sample the bronzed shrimp Creole, or do research for a restaurant review. Don't waste time perusing the intricacies of the menu. Don't ask the waiter how anything is prepared. Don't ask the waitress if a rasher of bacon is three strips or four. Food is not the focus – the customer is!"

Order something easy to eat. Order only one course. Order something inexpensive.

It is OK if you don't eat anything. It is rude to talk with food in your mouth. It is impolite to survey your dish when your customer is talking. And it is hard to take notes with a fork in your hand." [24]

Once the agenda is set I then prepare the presentation. Most customers are happy to have someone else prepare the presentation for a meeting because it means less work for them and it also allows you to control the content of the presentation. Where most salespeople miss the mark is making presentations slides that are confusing, contain information not pertinent to the discussion, contain too much information, or don't support the main point. I practice the "power of 3". I try to use only 3 bullet points on a slide, have 3 main points to my presentation and have only 3 action items at the end of the presentation. I also understand that I need to have only one most important take away from the presentation and realize that many people may only remember this one point.

Here is an example of action items I presented at the end of a presentation to one of my customers, the power of 3;

2018 Opportunities- rotors, transmissions, Dorman, slack adjusters, Delco Remy, DPF, tensioners and belts- Preferred Vendor

2018 Outlook- Bid Awards

Save $28,080,000- Increased Business

Earlier in the presentation I went up to the white board and wrote this figure; $20,080,000.00.

I then proceeded to show them that if I could save only half of their maintenance locations 3 days of down time per week at a cost of only $450 per day, I would save them $20,080,000.00 a year (all figures very conservative and realistic). This got their attention, especially considering that they spent a little under $6,000,000.00 with my firm. I then walked them through the logic of the savings and we discussed that down time was a major issue with their operation (remember uncovering a problem your customer doesn't even know they have and solving it?). Throughout the presentation this was my 1 main takeaway that I emphasized and included it in my action items.

Simplicity is a key in preparing any presentation, I prepare a 3 page per slide handout that I put notes on that I can refer to during the presentation and I take additional notes on during the discussion.

In your opening you want to evoke an emotion by using a bold image. Grab their attention and make them wonder what you are going to say next.

What 1 thing do you want the audience to remember?

It's not the "thing", it's

...the experience.

Bleed the image to the edge of the slide and make sure the image is facing the text, this is the natural way your eyes will move when looking at the image.

This image is facing the wrong way and the image is too small. Compare the two slides.

"Ask not what your country can do for you; ask what you can do for your country."

This slide is too busy. This should be a handout.

SALES RESULTS / PLAN

		CY					FY				
		2014	2015		2016		2014	2015		2016	
		Actual	Actual		Plan		Actual	Actual		Plan	
Dealer	Conv	5,445	6,079	11.6%	7,150	17.6%	5,556	6,360	14.5%	7,209	13.3%
	COE	1,229	1,776	44.5%	2,300	29.5%	1,366	2,046	49.8%	2,542	24.2%
		6,674	7,855	17.7%	9,450	20.3%	6,922	8,406	21.4%	9,751	16.0%
Natl Acct	Conv	398	1,256	215.6%	1,500	19.4%	869	1,321	52.0%	1,891	43.1%
	COE	3	72	2300.0%	550	663.9%	4	252	6200.0%	400	58.7%
		401	1,328	231.2%	2,050	54.4%	873	1,573	80.2%	2,291	45.6%
Wrecker	Conv	654	658	0.6%	650	-1.2%	698	613	-12.2%	700	14.2%
	COE	10	13	30.0%	0	-100.0%	10	14	40.0%	0	-100.0%
		664	671	1.1%	650	-3.1%	708	627	-11.4%	700	11.6%
PTL	Conv	1,384	1,378	-0.4%	1,500	8.5%	1,493	1,252	-16.1%	1,500	19.8%
	COE	84	58	-31.0%	200	244.3%	39	186	376.9%	238	28.0%
		1,468	1,436	-2.2%	1,700	18.4%	1,532	1,438	-6.1%	1,738	20.3%
TTL	Conv	7,881	9,371	18.9%	10,800	15.2%	8,616	9,546	10.8%	11,300	18.4%
	COE	1,326	1,919	44.7%	3,050	58.9%	1,419	2,498	76.0%	3,180	27.3%
		9,207	11,290	22.6%	13,850	22.7%	10,035	12,044	20.0%	14,480	20.2%

This slide it much too wordy, it should also be a handout. People will start reading it and they can read faster than you can talk, and people cannot read and listen effectively at the same time.

NATIONAL ACCOUNT FOCUS

Major National Accounts – Top 200 (ATT, Staples, Sysco, Pepsi, Frito Lay)
- Continue to support and conquest large National Accounts from our top 200 list
- Maintain and support national rental and leasing fleets (PTL, Ryder, ERAT)

Regional Accounts
- National Accounts to work closely with RVP's and DSM's to identify and prioritize markets with high potential i.e. Chicago, Indianapolis, Salt Lake City, etc
- Analyze available Polk Data for these markets to identify fleets with 100 plus units in our competitive set
- Begin actively calling on and selling these accounts in coordination with RVP's and DSM's
- RVP's and DSM's will be critical in determining which dealers will be used to facilitate and assist in the management of these deals
- Focus will be to identify highest potential for success such as underperforming markets and regional fleets not properly cultivated

Remember the "Power of 3".

The Power of 3

- **Listen**

- **Smile**

- **Seek to Understand**

Some other important things about presentations. I do not use transitions or other effects in my slides as they distract from my main point. In PPT you can press the B key to go to a black screen or the W key to go to a white screen. Be sure to spell check and check your figures and consistently use the same font on your slides. Don't get too caught up in making a flashy presentation, remember what you are trying to convey. Remember it's not about you it's about your customer.

The book *Presentation Zen* by Garr Reynolds is a great resource for creating and delivering impactful presentations. He gives some great points for making the most of your presentation design.

Remove all nonessential elements. Remove visual clutter. Avoid 3D effects.

People remember visuals better than bullet points.

Use high quality photos.

Repeat selected elements throughout your slide. You do not need to put your company logo on each slide. [2]

For a funny example of what not to do with Power Point watch the video *Life After Death by Power Point* by comedian Don McMillan.

It is very important to relax and be in the moment. Don't be thinking about anything else except the customer you are presenting to. Don't be thinking about your next meeting, what you are going to say next or what you are doing after work. Look at your customer, pick up on non-verbal cues and make eye contact. Your enthusiasm will carry over to your customer. Be sure that when you are talking that you are not looking behind you at your presentation but looking at the customer. Practice, practice, practice, believe in what you are selling, and it will show.

Now that you have your agenda and your presentation you need to practice. There is no substitution for practicing. I practice in a mirror and make sure that when I am talking I am looking at myself in the mirror, this means that I will be talking to my customer when I make the presentation. I arrive early, about 30 minutes early. This gives me several advantages: I may have time to meet additional company employees, I sometimes have time to 'look around' at displays, plaques, newsletters and find out what is important to this customer. I am often escorted into the meeting room early, so I can determine the best place for me to sit and the best place for my customer(s) to sit. If you can, be sure you arrange the seating, so your customer can look at you or look at the wall, if the customer can look out the window they will and that will be one more distraction to compete with. It also gives me additional time to work out any technical difficulties ahead of the presentation. When you set up and make your presentation be sure to eliminate barriers between you and the customer, like standing behind a table or lectern. You want to get close to your audience.

Now you are ready for the meeting to begin. You've done your homework and you have practiced your presentation. Remember what you goal is and what main takeaway you want your customer to remember.

Be sure to enthusiastically greet each customer as they enter the room with a smile and a firm handshake, looking them in the eye. Your appearance is important and a rule of thumb that I use is to dress as nice as the best dressed person I will meet with that day. Smile and be yourself. Relax your shoulders, hands at your side, move around the room but don't pace. Be sure to make eye contact with members of the audience during your presentation. You will make mistakes, but it is not brain surgery so no one is going to die.

I schedule regular business review meetings with my customers. I make sure that I have new information to share and a compelling reason for them to purchase my product or service.

Chapter 5

*Protect the Mother Lode, Take
Care of Yourself*

I have never seen a chapter like this in any of the many dozens of sales books that I have read so I decided to write this chapter first since it is pivotal to your success. I have seen too many salespeople jeopardize their health by not taking care of themselves. Many salespeople have hectic days with early mornings, travel, meetings, proposals, more travel and late nights with more meetings or answering emails and working on proposals in your hotel room. I have had more of those days than not but still managed to protect the mother lode. You can't take care of business until you first take care of yourself.

I was recently at a national sales meeting in Orlando and looking around the room I was struck by what I saw; many people who were very overweight and many who had already developed health problems because of their lifestyle. My hope is that I can motivate some of these people to start taking better care of themselves.

I have worked for companies where the prevailing culture was late nights and lots of alcohol. I worked for a firm where a supervisor would regularly say after having dinner and drinks, "just one more". Of course, it was never just one more as the supervisor and some of the other employees would then go out to the wee hours of the morning and come to the next morning's meeting gulping coffee, looking terrible and being totally unproductive. This is a terrible precedent for a supervisor to set. I have also seen this behavior lead to more than one DUI and other poor decisions for an employee, some career ending.

I was at a national sales meeting in Cleveland and one of our salespeople got so intoxicated that when someone pulled a prank and knocked on his hotel room door he came out into the hall way in his tightie whities without his key and the door closed behind him. Rather than going to the front desk he simply laid down in the hallway at the base of his hotel room door and fell asleep. He was still there when the early breakfast crowd started filtering in and he lost his job and had a hell of a hangover. It seems like there is always one person at these large meetings that will do something that they will spend a lot of time and energy trying to live down.

I attended another national sales manager's meeting in Chicago and knew that after the meeting my company's president would name the top contributor to the meeting and that person would get their picture taken with the president along with the recognition of standing out at the meeting. The district managers, regional directors and other company executives arrived the afternoon before and we all met for a cocktail reception that evening. I knew from previous meetings that many of my colleagues would have a few too many and would be nursing a hangover the next day. In order not to stick out or seem like I was not participating in the festivities I asked the bar tender to get me a soda and put it in a cocktail glass, so it looked like a cocktail. The next morning, I got up early and worked out at the hotel gym prior to the meeting. Many of my colleagues were struggling the next day. I remember looking around the room and seeing many of them slumped in their chairs trying to look invisible hoping no one would call on them or ask them a question. I was energized by the meeting, asked several questions and volunteered when questions were posed to the group. As you might have guessed I was named the most valuable participant at the meeting of about 50 and had my picture taken with the company president. The president and the other top executives were grateful for my participation. Looking back, I realized I was not the smartest guy in the room or the best communicator, but I had a big advantage over most people in the room, I simply took care of myself the night before.

I was at a company wide sales meeting in Atlantic City and discovered that the hotel charged $25 to use the gym each day. I went to my supervisor and asked if the company would cover the charges and was told no. I pointed out that the company would provide me with unlimited alcohol and food at the evenings dinner but would not pay me to stay healthy leading to a more productive meeting the next day. Many would overindulge and struggle to participate and contribute to the meeting the next day. The supervisor finally agreed, and I got a great workout in a very nice hotel gym and was very alert and productive during the next day's meetings.

Most companies do little to help you take care of yourself outside of a health insurance plan and maybe a health risk assessment. Some companies do provide discounts for health club memberships, company funded weight loss, nutrition and smoking cessation programs. Take advantage of whatever health benefits you can to protect the mother lode.

General Motors operated a nice gym in a large office headquarters building where I worked. The gym included group exercise classes along with cardio equipment, free weights, locker room and showers. I worked out at lunch 3-5 times per week. It was a great stress reliever and broke up the day nicely. It was also a great place to network as you got to know the regular workout crowd.

HOW DO I PROTECT THE MOTHER LODE?

The most difficult time for me to protect the mother lode is when I am on the road. The temptation of fast food, late dinners with clients, open bars at meetings, sitting on a plane or sitting in the car for hours, it all adds up. I had to create new habits to take care of myself. I started keeping track of the calories in the foods that I ate and once it became a habit it was easy and kept me healthy.

In his book *The Power of Habit* Charles Duhigg has shown that habits are formed by a loop of cue, routine and reward.

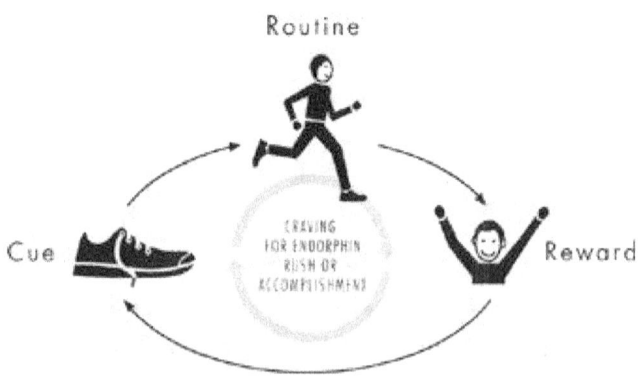

[1]

"Researchers have learned that cues can be almost anything, from a visual trigger such as a candy bar or a television commercial to a certain place, a time of day, an emotion, a sequence of thoughts, or a company of particular people. Routines can be incredible complex or fantastically simple (some habits, such as those related to emotions, are measured in milliseconds). Rewards can range from food or drugs that cause physical sensations, to emotional payoffs, such as the feelings of pride that accompany praise or self-congratulations".

"Habits are powerful, but delicate. They can emerge outside of our consciousness or can be deliberately designed. They often occur without our permission but can be reshaped by fiddling with their parts. They shape our lives far more than we realize -- they are so strong, in fact, that they cause our brains to cling to them at the exclusion of all else, including common sense". [1]

This explains some of the poor choices my colleagues made in the stories above. My **cue** for taking care of myself during sales meetings is the meeting notice or being at the event, the **routine** is not to overindulge in either food or alcohol and the **reward** is how good I will feel the next day, especially compared to some of my colleagues and the benefits I will get out the meetings because I am physically and mentally prepared.

Good news as Duhigg writes. "Anyone can use this basic formula to create habits of her or his own. Want to exercise more? Choose a cue, such as going to the gym as soon as you wake up, and a reward, such as a smoothie after each workout. Then think about that smoothie, or about the endorphin rush you'll feel. Allow yourself to anticipate the reward. Eventually, that craving will make it easier to push through the gym doors every day". [1]

So how do you change some bad habits? Duhigg states that you need to understand the needs that drive our behaviors.

"Say you want to stop snacking at work. Is the reward you're seeking to satisfy your hunger? Or is it to interrupt boredom? If you snack for a brief release, you can easily find another routine – such as taking a quick walk, or giving yourself three minutes on the Internet – that provides the same interruption without adding to your waistline." [1]

I try to get in a work out every morning when I am on the road. The cues I use are lacing up my running shoes or texting my wife that I am heading to the gym. She will send me a motivational text in return.

---- Jan 30 ----

6:37 AM **heading to gym lover.**

Work it stud. 8:30 AM

Have a great meeting.
Love you. Date night. 😉 9:17 AM

The routine usually starts with walking on the treadmill followed by weight training, running, biking, running the hotel stairs (my favorite) or other exercise depending on the hotel gym. The reward is being better prepared for the day and feeling great knowing I am doing everything I can to make myself successful. I sometimes will send her a picture after my workout to which she will give me another motivational reply.

(not bad for 60)

It helps when you include other people in your good habits. I also have a Garmin Vivo Fit and use it to track my daily steps. Since getting this I now will walk instead of sitting while waiting for a plane and often will walk on the treadmill at the hotel in the evening if I haven't reached my target steps for the day. I know that there are far more people that are not protecting the mother lode because most mornings when I go to the hotel gym I am the only one in the gym. I also notice that when I run the stairs and get above the 2nd floor the stairs become much cleaner because they go mostly unused.

Everyone can find some time to protect the mother lode. When I was a branch manager in the car rental business I used to work out at about 5:30 am every morning in my basement. It relieved stress and got me ready for the day. In that position the customers were often waiting at the door when the team arrived at work. I had already been up for a couple of hours and was energized to start the day, it made a big difference.

A study in the Journal of Medicine and Science in Sports and Exercise found that women who exercised in the morning were less distracted by delicious foods, increased their physical activity throughout the day and increased their metabolism thus burning more calories throughout the day. [11]

Eating well is just as important as exercise. Counting calories really helps but common sense works too. Choose the salmon vs. the steak, skip the fries and get a side salad, get the small portion and skip the soda and choose water. I keep a journal of the things that I eat and their calories. I don't restrict many foods, but I have a limit on the calories I consume each day. It is surprisingly easy to do, even on the road, and you can skip the pre-packaged meals or weight loss meetings. I also find myself eating healthier as I keep track of the foods that I put into my body. A good rule of thumb is all things in moderation, as the Greek poet **Hesiod** (c.700 B.C.) wrote, 'observe due measure; moderation is best in all things'.

I recently had a conversation with a co-worker who was over-weight and he had to go to the doctor because of a foot infection and found out that he is now diabetic. It struck me when he hung his head and said, "I didn't take care of myself, it's my own fault."

Some good news for those getting a little older, as Dr. Bob Arnot lays out in his book, *Dr. Bob Arnot's Guide to Turning Back the Clock*. Dr. Bob points out the difference between conventional wisdom and the new paradigm.

Conventional Wisdom;

Go with the flow.

New Paradigm;

Aging is a cultural trap that programs men to abuse, misuse, and disuse their bodies.

"How many times have you wished to be eighteen again, taking back with you your wisdom, experience, knowledge, and your wallet? That trip back in time was science fiction a generation ago. Today, returning to your youth can be a reality. If you are between thirty and sixty you can crank back the time on your biological clock by a staggering amount as determined by standardized human-performance tests for biological age. What's changed? Dramatic breakthroughs in nutrition, fitness technology, and sports medicine. If the idea of dragging your body through a time warp seems like a pretty weird idea, be assured, it really works". [3]

And who benefits the most?

Any man who doesn't practice optimum nutrition.

Sedentary men.

Aerobically fit men who have never built any muscle.

Muscularly fit men who are aerobically unfit.

More good news is that it all works, but you must be disciplined enough to use it consistently just like a sales plan.

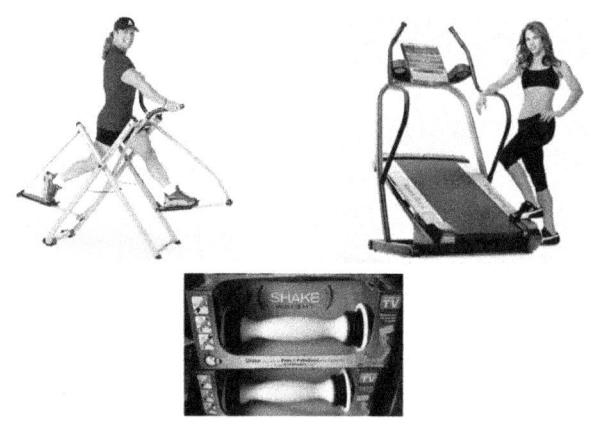

As I get a little older I also concentrate more on reducing my stress. I believe that stress is the cause of many health problems. I have done meditation and yoga and it all works if you use it on a regular basis. I have always put more stress on myself than any supervisor that I have ever had.

When reflecting on one's life no one ever says, "I wished I had spent more time working", but I have heard many people say, "I wished I had taken better care of myself."

Once you start you can make it a habit to protect the mother lode!

Chapter 6

Negotiating and Closing the Sale

There are some basic rules to follow in any negotiation.

Do your homework before you sit down to deal. Learn as much as you can about the people and company you are negotiating with. Do not rely on your instincts. Have the facts to make your case.

Never negotiate with yourself. Once you have made an offer, if it is not accepted, do not make another offer without getting a counter offer. You will not know where the other party stands without hearing their offer.

Negotiate with the decision maker(s), not someone who has to "go back and talk to the boss". This wastes time and you will be negotiating twice.

If you are negotiating an agreement be sure you read the entire agreement. I have negotiated contracts that had already been reviewed and edited by both side's legal teams, but I was still responsible for negotiating the final details.

Few negotiators will tell you their whole story up front. It is up to you to determine what is most important to them. Ask questions and listen. Get the other party to tell you what their needs are.

Few things are non-negotiable. You won't know until you ask. Negotiate on the minor issues. If you give a concession always ask, "If we make it happen, do we have the order today?"

Tell a story to get the other party excited. Show the other party the benefits of doing business with you and the cost of not doing business with you. Monetize the options.

When we negotiate we need to put ourselves in the other party's shoes, ask questions and understand what is most important to them. I have an exercise that I conduct that highlights the above rules

I give one person the seller's scenario and the other the buyer's scenario. The buyer has $5 and after the final negotiation the buyer and seller get to keep the amount they negotiated for. Neither team knows the other sides confidential information and they are not able to divulge this confidential information during the negotiation. If a deal is not reached, then the money is returned. It helps to have an actual product and I pick up various items at a local one-dollar retailer.

The Negotiation- Seller

Confidential Information;

Your company is suffering financial difficulties and ideally, you should sell your product for $5. Anything less and the company will have to lay off staff. The minimum sale price of $3 is the break-even value of your product.

You know your product well and all about the product warranty, shipping, packaging, etc.…. It is imperative that you sell the product as you need the cash flow now and will lose money every day that the product sits on your shelves.

The Negotiation- Buyer

You have been offered a similar product from another company A for $2 and so cannot go any higher. You will look good in your boss's eyes if you can get the product for $2 and your boss is looking at you for a promotion. Nevertheless, you have been a client of the seller for 10 years and want to give the seller a chance to make the sale. The company that offered the service for $2 was not able to provide a shipping schedule or specifics on the warranty, but you don't want to share this information with the seller unless specifically asked.

Confidential Information;

It is imperative that you buy this product now as you may lose customers if you cannot provide this product now.

This is a fun exercise that teaches participants how much they do not know about the motivations of the other side in negotiations. The more questions you ask and the more you listen the more you learn. In this scenario the seller has an 'in' if they ask questions about shipping and product warranty, which is a need of the buyer.

I have heard that if your first offer isn't enough to make the other side laugh then it wasn't strong enough. I am not sure this is the best advice, but you do have to start somewhere. The sooner you find out where your customer stands the sooner you can work on your solution. You can either get your customer to make the first offer or get your customer to counter offer your proposal.

In negotiating, the side that holds the power is usually the side that 'thinks' they have the power. You can negotiate from a position of power if you are ok with walking away from the negotiation without a deal. The party that 'has to' make a deal usually feels as though they have none of the power in a negotiation. Power is perception and if you think you don't have it then you don't. I have walked away from several negotiations only to have the other party come back with a sweeter deal.

An illustration of the power of perception is a neighbor of mine, John, who was a champion miler (one-mile runner). He has won dozens and dozens of races and has a trove of trophies. He told me that when he got up to the starting line he would look at the other runners, most of whom he knew well. He would say to himself, "I worked harder than he did", "I trained smarter than he did", "I ran more miles that he did", convincing himself that he was more prepared and thus had an edge over the rest of the field. This may have been true for some of the competition, but it didn't matter because John had convinced himself that he was going to win the race, which he almost always did. He had won the race before it started, the power of perception.

Another factor in negotiation in called BATNA. Best Alternative to a Negotiated Agreement. If you reach an impasse and are not able to reach an agreement, what next? A smart negotiator will have thought of the possibility of no agreement and have a plan B. Maybe there is an alternative agreement, partial agreement or shorter-term agreement that can be reached. Ask you customer what their BATNA is, this lets them know that this is something you have thought about and may give you some perceived power in the negotiation. The answer to this question will also give you an idea if your customer has thought about their BATNA and if they know what their strategy is. Your customer might not have a BATNA or their BATNA puts them in a worse position than reaching an agreement with you. Again, you won't know unless you ask.

I was watching an episode of 'American Pickers' and Mike was interested in an item, but the owner said it wasn't for sale. Mike asked him for his 'don't want to sell price'. The owner gave him a price and that was the starting point in the negotiating. The item actually was for sale as long as the owner was getting a price he perceived as fair. Again, you will not know what is negotiable unless you ask.

In the book, *Never Split the Difference*, *Negotiating as if Your Life Depended on it,* author, Chris Voss, a former FBI international, kidnaping negotiator relates the skills learned in the FBI negotiating with bank robbers and international criminal organizations to the world or business. The authors emphasizing the importance of listen in negotiating. "It all starts with the universally applicable premise that people want to be understood and accepted. Listening is the cheapest, yet most effective concession we can make to get there. By listening intensely, a negotiator demonstrates empathy and shows sincere desire to better understand what the other side is experiencing."

"Psychotherapy research shows that when individuals feel listened to, they tend to listen to themselves more carefully and to openly evaluate and clarify their own thoughts and feelings. In addition, they tend to become less defensive and oppositional and more willing to listen to other points of view, which gets them to the calm and logical place where they can be good *Getting to Yes* problem solvers." [12]

Chris discusses several key strategies and tactics for effective negotiating including the following;

Lose Aversion. Keep in mind that statistically averting a loss is riskier that realizing an equal gain to most people. What is the cost to the customer of not doing business with you? Identify it and monetize it.

Mirroring. Mirroring is something we do much of the time, if we realize it or not. When you are talking to someone if they smile you smile. If they fold their arms you tend to fold your arms. If they nod you begin to nod. "It's almost laughably simple: for the FBI, a 'mirror' is when you repeat the last three words (or the critical one to three words) of what someone has just said. Of the entirety of the FBI's hostage negotiation skill set, mirroring is the closest one gets to a Jedi mind trick. Simple, and yet uncannily effective." [12]

Labeling. Sometimes emotions are strained in a negotiation and get in the way of reaching an agreement. Chris talks about labeling those emotions to more effectively deal with them. "That's why, instead of denying or ignoring emotions, good negotiators identify them. They are able to precisely label emotions, those of others and especially their own. And once they label the emotions they talk about them without getting wound up. For them, emotions are a tool." [12]. If you see emotions surface during negotiations you can discuss them and deal with them by asking questions like, I can see you don't agree with that statement, what don't you agree with? You could also ask, it appears this part of the proposal is not acceptable, what could we change to make it work for you? Keep your head up and eyes open to verbal and non-verbal cues during negotiations.

Tactical Empathy. "Tactical empathy is understanding the feelings and mindset of another in the moment and also hearing what is *behind* those feelings so you increase your influence in all the moments that follow." [12]. Again, it's not about you.

Emotional intelligence. Daniel Goleman describes what emotion intelligence is, why it matters and how to use it in life and business in his book, *Emotional Intelligence; Why it can matter more than IQ*. Emotional intelligence includes emotional awareness including the ability to identify emotions in others as well as yourself. Emotional intelligence also is the ability to control or manage your emotions and not let them get in the way of your personal or business relationships. The ability to harness your emotions, keep calm and stay on task is another important element of emotional intelligence. People with high emotional intelligence can put themselves in someone else's shoes and show empathy. People with high emotional IQ are accepting of their own strengths and weaknesses and because of this are not afraid to ask questions to get clarification and learn. [28]

The difference between high IQ and high emotional IQ is highlighted by Malcolm Gladwell in his book, *Outliers; The Story of Success*. Malcolm tells the story of Christopher Langan, who has been called the smartest man in American. Christopher has an IQ of 195, compare that to the IQ of Albert Einstein which was 160. Christopher is a celebrity of sorts appearing on a game show and being the subject of several articles and a documentary film, but Christopher did not achieve the success you would expect from the smartest man in America. He didn't find the cure for cancer, invent a miracle product or start the most successful company every. Because of his low emotional IQ, what he did was work as a bouncer for 20 years and worked as a farm hand and a forest service ranger. Thinking about it these jobs limited interaction with people or the interactions were scripted. As a farm hand you work mostly with animals and as a forest service ranger trees. The requirement for emotion IQ was low or non-existent in these jobs. [29]

Accusation Audit. "The first step of doing so is listing every terrible thing your counterpart *could* say about you, in what I call an accusation audit." [12]. In the movie *8 Mile*, Eminem was about to go onstage for a rap battle and he knew the other rapper would make fun of him for being white, living in a mobile home and being poor. Eminem's friend suggested he include all of that in his own rap, thus taking all the ammo away from his competitor. It worked as the other rapper really didn't have anything negative to say about Eminem, it had already been said. "Performing an accusation audit in advance prepares you to head off negative dynamics before they take root. And because these accusations often sound exaggerated when said aloud, speaking them will encourage the other person to claim that quite the opposite is true." [12]

Don't be afraid of 'NO'- "We have it backward. For good negotiators, No is pure gold. That negative provides a great opportunity for you and the other party to clarify what you really want by eliminating what you don't want. No is a safe choice that maintains the status quo; it provides a temporary oasis of control.". "Saying no gives the speaker the feeling of safety, security, and control. You use a question that prompts a No answer, and your counterpart feels that by turning you down he has proven that he's in the driver's seat. Good negotiators welcome – even invite – a solid No to start, as a sign that the other party is engaged and thinking." [12].

How do you come back from a "No"? A "No" means many things but it does not mean the negotiation is over, quite the opposite it is just beginning. No could mean "I am not ready to purchase yet", or "I don't really understand the specifics of your offer", or "No, I don't want to buy from you". The sale professional will ask the questions that get the reasons to these hidden answers. When will you ready to place the order? What don't you understand about the proposal? And, why are you thinking about rewarding the business to someone else? You will not get every sale, but you will learn from every sales interaction.

Closing the Sale.

There are many gimmick closes and even books written about them. But, you have done your homework, asked the right questions and prepared your proposal, do you really want to start using gimmicks now? There is an old adage that once you close the deal, stop talking, shake hands, get up and leave. Not altogether bad advice but often closing the deal is not that simple.

In his book *In Business As In Life – You Don't Get What You Deserve, You Get What You Negotiate,* author Chester L. Karrass talks about closing. "Settlement generally occurs when each party believes that the agreement close at hand offers greater satisfaction than no agreement. The agreement is perceived as better than other available alternatives, and each side believes that the other has conceded most of what it will. Both believe that further effort spent negotiating is not worthwhile." [30]

Following most of the negotiations I have been a part of it was obvious when it was time to close. For those times when you are not sure or want to move ahead with closing I use the following questions.

What do you suggest we do? How do you propose we do that? Include your customer in the solution.

Why don't you try it, return it if you don't like it? Companies that provide product returns usually get back less than 1/10 of 1% of sales.

I think you have already decided to move ahead, am I right?

Do you have any other questions before we move forward?

Why don't you place a smaller order now and see how that goes?

Keep your head up and look for non-verbal clues and body language. If you have followed the steps of a successful salesperson the close will likely be anticlimactic.

Chapter 7

Lessons From Wile E. Coyote

When I was a kid I watched the Road Runner cartoons and was amused at how the Road Runner would always outsmart the Coyote. Wile E. Coyote, however, has many attributes of a successful salesperson. He has a clear goal, never gives up, tries new methods and technologies, takes personal, often painful, responsibility for his failures, has a positive attitude, smiles (smirks), has patience and never seems to try a failed technique twice. You must admire his GRIT, his ability to work towards a long-term goal regardless of the obstacles put in his place.

So why doesn't he succeed?

He underestimates the Road Runner. The Road Runner is fast, his best attribute, and Wile E. Coyote seems to come up with a plan to overcome the speed but underestimates the cunning and instincts of the Road Runner.

He uses only one supplier. Acme may be a good supplier and their products may work as advertised but they may not be the best fit for Wile E. Coyote.

Wile E. Coyote does not improve every year. He doesn't take corrective action based on his failures. If he did a self-assessment he would realize that he needs to change his methods and techniques.

Wile E. Coyote goes it alone. He knows he needs help but doesn't consult outside sources or experts to improve his chance of success. He always thinks that he has the best ideas.

Don't be Wile E. Coyote.

Chapter 8

Mistakes Salespeople Make

One of the biggest mistakes that salespeople make is they **talk too much**. I have known a few salespeople that always had stories to tell and people would say they had the gift of gab. The only people impressed by them or thought they had the right stuff were other salespeople who mistakenly thought that was the way you sold something. Customers were not impressed. Salespeople who show up and chew the fat or 'visit' are tolerated but not appreciated.

Many salespeople do what is known as "show up and throw up," or bombard a customer with features and benefits without knowing what the customer really wants. This is a result of not asking the right questions and not listening to the customer.

Salespeople **don't smile enough**. "There is a saying, 'Frown and you frown alone, but smile and the whole world smiles with you.' From the moment we are born we learn that smiling is the fastest way to get others to pay attention to us. A baby's smile lights up the room. Smiles attract. Frowns repel. Even dogs understand this. A wagging tail, an upturned mouth, and bright, wide eyes are the fastest route to a pat or a treat." [6] I have seen dozens of parents holding babies when traveling. When you smile at a baby they immediately smile back, it is engrained in all of us since birth. Smile and you are seen as a friend. In his TED talk, researcher Ron Gutman discusses the many benefits of smiling. Research has shown that people who smile more live longer, heathier, happier and more fulfilling lives. One study showed that the span of a person's smile can actually predicted the span of their life. Children smile about 400 times a day and only 1/3 of adults smile more than 20 times a day. Smiling is an evolutionary contagion meaning when you smile people will smile back. Smiling also decreases stress reducing hormones and lowers your blood pressure. When you smile others view you as more likeable, better looking, courteous and more competent. If you want to close more sales, smile ☺. (http://www.ted.com/talks/ron_gutman_the_hidden_power_of_smiling) [16]

Salespeople mistakenly **think that price is the most important thing to a customer**. Study after study shows that price is not most important to customers and is not even in the top 5 of things customers want. Here is what customer say they want most;

Solutions to their problems

Fast response

Product availability

Quality

Courteous, honest, sincerely cheerful sales people

There is a saying, that the sweetness of low price is quickly forgotten by the bitterness of low quality and poor service.

"When the topic of price comes up, a powerful technique is for the sales professional to shift the discussion from price to value. The value of a current offering is a great place to start this dialogue. During the course, of such a discussion, it is useful to get the customer to rank the elements of the offering in order of importance. This sometimes enables the customer to see the offering in a different light; these new insights are very useful to both the sales professional and the customer as they think about value." [8]

Often when the topic of price comes up it is a default topic because you have nothing else to talk about. "Your job is to provide information that elevates the conversation beyond the cost associated with your product or service. You must educate your prospects about potential outcomes that transcend your product or service. This may be the added value or a tangible return on investment that the client receives beyond the product itself." [7]

I have never worked for a low-price company and I never will. In fact, I have worked for companies that were price leaders. In these companies we controlled the market pricing. When we raised our price so did our competitors and when we lowered our price our competitors followed suit. We were the leaders not the followers. I talk about price up front with many of my customers. I remove it as an obstacle early in the sales process. When someone says, "your price is too high." There are several things you need to know and questions you need to ask.

Compared to what? Are we comparing apples to apples or a name brand to a cheap generic product?

What do you include in the price of a product? On time delivery, fast, personal assistance, longer service life, best warranty, help solving your problems, rebates, volume discounts, etc....

We have the lowest total cost. Do your homework and know what you do well and what your competition does well/poorly. Prove it with statistic or a white paper.

We could lower our price, what benefits would you be willing to give up? There is a cost to lower prices. Why do you think the competitor is cheaper? What are they not offering?

I had a great salesperson that worked for me that sold large RVs. When he was struggling to close a sale, Justin would say to the customer, "there are 1 of 3 reasons why you don't want to buy this RV today. You don't like the RV, and in that case, I have over 100 other RVs we can look at. You don't like the price, and in that case, I can talk to my manager about a discount or you don't like me. Well the customer would immediately say that they liked Justin so that narrowed it to 2 reasons and the customer would offer up the reason for their hesitation. This really worked for Justin to move the sale forward.

Another mistake is **thinking that sales is all or nothing**. I have always told my salespeople that it is not that bad to be #2 with a customer. Eventually, #1 will stumble and then you will be in position to move up to #1. I have also told them that they do not need to be the best salesperson in the world, just better than the competitor's salesperson. Getting a 'no' from a customer is not the end, it is the beginning. You learn something from every sales contact and can build on that for the next sales contact. What lessons did you learn? Be sure to write it down. If you get a 'no' does the customer know of someone else who could benefit from your product or service? Get a referral.

In their book *Never Split the Difference*, Chris Voss and Tahl Taz talk about getting a 'no'. "One negotiating genius who's impossible to miss is Mark Cuban, the billionaire owner of the Dallas Mavericks. I always quote to my students one of his best lines on negotiating: "Every 'No' gets me closer to a 'Yes.'" [12]

A common mistake is **thinking that your top accounts are solid**. How do you know? Your top accounts are your competitor's top prospects. They may be your top accounts, but do you know their potential? They may be your competitors top account too. With one company I worked for my top account was also my competitor's top account and my competitor was getting much more of the business than I was. I found this out because one of my fellow employees had worked for the competitor. I was originally asking for a purchase increase of about 6% but eventually asked for over 100% once I found out their potential.

Never **think a customer is small change**. How do you know? I have had large and small accounts and I never ignored my smaller accounts like many of my colleagues. I have taken over sales territories and customer told me that they had not seen a representative from our company for 25 years, 25 years! These customers really appreciated me calling on them and it showed in the increased business that I got. This payed off big for me.

I had big accounts that were doing 95% to 99% of objective but my small accounts would be at 155% to 169% of objective, putting me over 100% of my sales objective. At a truck OE I worked for it was a major milestone when a customer purchased a million dollars in a year, we would present them with a plaque and acknowledge their achievement in our newsletter and at our annual meetings. When I started with the company we did not have any customers purchasing a million dollars but after just a few years we had dozens of customers in that category. Many of the customers we thought would easily reach the one- million-dollar mark didn't and many customers we thought never would, reached it easily.

When I was a salesperson at a lumber company I witnessed the salespeople rushing to help the customer that drove into the lot in a big truck. They were all hoping the customer would buy enough lumber and supplies to fill up the truck. Often the customer just wanted a box of nails or tool to finish the job. I would greet and help all customers and I remember one day when a man drove up in a beat up old car and ordered an entire two car garage, door, windows, siding, roofing, he ordered it all.

Salespeople often **don't treat everyone with respect**. Everyone you come into contact with is important to your success. All customer employees and your company's employees can help or hurt you. From the receptionist and warehouse worker to the engineer and marketing specialist.

In an episode of the television show *Undercover Boss*, the CEO of 7-Eleven stores went to a location in Shirley, NY to find out why the location sold more coffee than any of the over 10,000 7-Eleven U.S. locations. The CEO soon discovered that it wasn't the store's location, special coffee or special pricing it was Dolores. Dolores was a grandmother who had worked for 7-Eleven for 18 years. What was her secret? She interacted and knew the names of all her regular customers. She greeted them and called them by name as they came in for coffee during her 5-10 am shift. Now wouldn't that be nice if you went to a store you frequented and were greeted by name and asked how you were doing? Do you do that with your customers?

[14]

A heart felt 'thank you' to the receptionist or a small token of your appreciation goes a long way. I had a customer that I always brought chocolate for when I called on them. My first visit to them was on Valentine's day and after that it became a habit to bring them chocolate. I always brought an extra and would give it to the receptionist. The receptionist was very appreciative and would always make sure we had water and went out of their way to help us.

Many salespeople **do not provide good service after the sale**. Astute business people know it is more expensive to get a new customer than to keep an existing customer. Many salespeople have time to prospect for new customers but not enough time to service the customers they already have. They also know that it is expensive to get back a customer that you have lost. Often there is mistrust and sometimes bad feelings with customers that you have lost. I have seen salespeople and companies lose very good customers over $50.

"One of the best times to serve outrageously is after the sale. This is a time when a customer may not be certain about his status. After all, you have already parted a fool and his money. That's why a personal thank you note or a telephone follow-up takes on extra meaning. You don't have to do it. There is not additional money in it for you. You must genuinely care. Amazing." [15]

"Let's get right to the truth: Service is an affair of the heart, because for service to touch the mind of the consumer it must come from the heart of the server. As Sally Field once said at the Academy Awards, "You like me, you really, really like me!" And that is the exact reaction that people feel when they are served outrageously." [15]

Follow up with customers, keep them in the loop concerning their project, order, request, etc.... Keep in contact with your customers and you will have a better chance of getting information on additional opportunities or learn of possible issues that will be easier to solve sooner rather than later. Sending your customer, a note on their birthday, anniversary or when they are in the news is a good time to stay in touch and much appreciated.

Salespeople **do not know how to handle complaining customers**. One reason salespeople and companies lose customers is they do not know how to handle disputes. What has worked for me for over 25 years is the following;

Feel- I know how you feel about the situation.

Felt- I would have felt the same way if it was me.

Find- Let's find a solution to this together.

I listen to the customer, telling them that I know how they **feel**, because I would have **felt** the same way if it had happened to me. I then **find** a solution with the customer. My goal is to keep them as a customer and I almost always got a commitment from the customer to use my company again.

There is an old saying in sales, "when customers complain, they are doing you a favor." Most salespeople don't get this and think a complaining customer is no more than a pain in the neck. A complaining customer gives you feedback and allows you to improve and solve problems. When I worked as a regional director in the car rental business I would deal with upset customers after they had already dealt with the rental agent, branch manager and district manager. You would think that their issue was major after having gone through that many levels. Well, it was surprising that after talking to many of these customers they only wanted someone to listen to them and not interrupt them or argue with them. Also, many of the issues revolved around one or two days of rental expense which was often under $50. The expense of time it cost my company to deal with these customers far exceeded the dollar amount of their issue. It would have been better for everyone, company and customer, if the rental agent had satisfied the customer on the spot. Often employees are too close to the situation or let personal feelings get in the way of making a smart decision. We instituted training for all front-line employees and empowered them to satisfy customers. This significantly decreased the amount of complaints that moved up the management chain and improved our level of customer service.

"According to the U.S. Office of Consumer Affairs, between 37 and 45 percent of people who are unhappy with service do not complain. They go elsewhere. That's not the worst of it, when you think about the average of thirteen potential customers they will influence with stories about how poor their treatment was. When you think about the customers in terms of both lifetime sales potential and their impact on others, almost anything you can do to save a customer is a bargain." [15]

Just as unhappy customers tell stories about poor service or poor products to their friends, happy customers tell stories of great service and great products. Ask your customers who else may benefit from your product or service. Ask for a referral.

Another mistake salespeople make is **not having a positive attitude**. There is a saying, "attitude is everything." I agree and have witnessed that you can overcome a lot of shortcomings by having a positive attitude. I have seen salespeople be more successful selling a bad promotion with a good attitude than selling a good promotion with a poor attitude. Not all the programs and promotions that I have been asked to sell were good, but I let the customer decide if it was good for them. I watched salespeople make the decision that it was a bad program before they started selling it and they were never successful. Not every program or promotion is for everyone but let the customer make that decision.

Jeb Blount talks about something closely related to a positive attitude, likeability. "*People Buy You* begins and ends with likability because being likable and remaining likable is sort of like "relationship glue." Likability impacts how other perceive you, their willingness to engage in conversation, and their openness to answering your questions. In addition, it affects their desire to give you second chances when inevitable mistakes and service issues occur. Likability makes the difference in how you and your message are received by others. Without it, you simply cannot and will not connect with others." [6]

"Enthusiasm is simply having excitement for or interest in what you are doing. What we have already learned about human nature is that people respond in kind. If you are enthusiastic about something, it is likely that those around you will become enthusiastic, too. The good news is we generally find enthusiastic people likeable, and we are more likely to accept their point of view. This is why enthusiasm is such an important tool for salespeople. There is an old saying, "A salesperson without enthusiasm is just a clerk." [5]

Another mistake salespeople make is **they don't answer their phone**. People want to talk to people. Customers do not want to send a request to help@XYZcompany.com or go into your company's voice maze. Everything else that a salesperson does won't matter if the customer can't get ahold of you when they need you. I know that every salesperson has other things going on each day, but if you are not available be sure your customer knows it is because you are with another customer. The only thing worse than your customer not being able to get ahold of you when they need you is the reason you give them for not being available. Your customer does not want to hear that you were at a company retreat, on a company conference call or in a company budget meeting. Customers do understand that you have other clients and that you give these clients the same attention that you give them. I have seen many salespeople look at their ringing phone and say, I'll call them back. Answer your phone. I never turn my phone off and rarely get after hours calls, but when I do I can hear the appreciation in the voice of my customer that they were able to get ahold of me when they needed some help.

Many salespeople **do not have proper goals**. What I mean by proper goals are those that are S.M.A.R.T. Specific, measurable, attainable, relevant and on a timetable. I would add that you need to write them down. A company I worked for had an annual customer trip and the top salesperson also attended. The company printed a nice full color brochure with pictures and information about the host country. I would take that brochure and hang it on the wall of my office. Going on that trip was one of my annual goals and something that I would look at every day that I was in my office. It worked as I enjoyed several trips to international locations.

In his book, *What They Don't Teach You at Harvard Business School,* Mark McCormack discusses a 1979 study in which new Harvard MBA graduates were asked one question, "Have you set clear, written goals for your future and have you made plans to accomplish them?" Only three percent of the graduates had both written goals and plans, 13 percent had goals but had not written them down and 84 percent had no clear goals.

A follow up study was done ten years later with the respondents. The 13 percent of the class who had goals but not in writing had average earnings of twice as much as the 84 percent who had no clear goals. The 3 percent who had clear, written goals had average earnings of ten times as much as the other 97 percent put together. [17]

Goals need to be **specific**, i.e. I want to achieve $33,459,195 in sales this year. Not, I want to sell a lot more than I did last year. Goals need to be **measurable**, i.e. my goal is to hold quarterly business review meetings (4x per year) with each of my customers, not I would like to get to know my customers better. Goals should be **attainable,** i.e. I would like to increase my sales by 11%, or $4,295,147 this year, not I would like to increase my sales by 1,000 % with each of my customers this year. Goals need to be **relevant,** i.e. I would like to complete 3 of the 4 sales training modules by July 1, not I would like to visit one interesting place in each of the states I cover. Goals need to have a **timetable**, i.e. I would like my sales to equal $3,245,115 by the end of the first quarter by March 31, not I would like to launch vendor training modules 1-2 when it feels right.

Got goals? Write them down.

Chapter 9

Sales Leadership

I manage problems and lead people. There is a difference between managing and leading. A wise salesperson once told me, Tom, I will follow a leader but never a boss. If you don't have better ideas, work harder, care about the people that you work with and appreciate what you have more than the people you lead, then you have no business leading people. Most bosses don't get the first rule of sales and leadership, it's not about you!

I had a sales manager tell a story about the expensive patio they just installed with a $5,000 outdoor grill. I had another sales manager tell a story about their very expensive $4,500 smart refrigerator. Nice stories but not ones a leader should be telling their sales staff. The sales staff was unimpressed because they work hard every day and still didn't want to spend $5,000 on an outdoor grill or refrigerator. The thought that most of the sales team had was that these people are grossly overpaid if that's what they spend their money on and then brag about it. These managers will never become leaders until they understand the first rule, it's not about them.

In a 2018 Gallup Poll study 34% of American workers were engaged, an all-time high. While 53% were not engaged (show up for work and do the minimum required) and 13% were actively disengaged (have miserable work experiences). This is mostly because of poor management. [21]

Why are there so many bad managers out there? Is it because they think it is all about them? Is it because they don't understand that they get paid for what their sales staff does and not what they do? Is it because they have little to no management training? Is it because their ego grows when they get the title 'boss'? Or is it because they simply do not know what they are doing? The answer is yes, to all of the above.

Google is a great company that is incredibly profitable and a great place to work, but they were having a hard time holding onto their employees. To this end Google launched "Project Oxygen", in 2009, to find out how to build a better boss. [18] Project Oxygen analyzed years of internal performance reviews, feedback surveys, employee complaints and nominations for top-manager rewards, while correlating phrases, words, complaints and praise. [19] After analyzing the qualitative data with over 10,000 observations of manager behavior Google created eight behaviors of great managers. Let's look at them in order of importance.

1. **Be a good coach**. If you watch an athletic coach, especially Hall of Fame, Men's basketball coach Tom Izzo of Michigan State you see that those he coaches get regular, tailored, specific, immediate feedback both positive and corrective. If one of Tom's players makes a mistake in a game they are often taken out of the game and are given a 'talking to' on their way to the bench. If one of Tom's players makes a good play, out hustles the opponent or dives for a loose ball you can see the supportive reaction of Tom on the sidelines. This is quite different than most managers in business. Employee reviews are usually preformed once or twice a year and most managers are very uncomfortable if they need to discuss anything negative or required corrective action. A good coach needs to give great feedback and needs to be available and approachable. Make time for regular one-on-one meetings with your staff. One of the most important roles of a coach is to remove obstacles for your staff, you solve their problems just like the salesperson solves the customer's problems.

2. **Empower your team and don't micromanage**. A great leader needs to know when to direct

their team and when to get out of their way. "No matter what business you're in, to be successful, managers must create the kind of environment that makes their people the most productive. It isn't enough to make them conscious of details if you destroy their sense of freedom and spontaneity in the process. You must understand them well enough to give them not what *you* want, but also what *they* need to make a maximum contribution." [20]. There is no better way to demoralize your sales team than to micromanage them. I have seen several micromanagers fail miserably suffering from low sales, high turnover and poor employee morale. A motivated employee will produce from 30-50% more than an unmotivated employee. My experience is it can be higher than 50%. Micromanagers are working harder and getting less done in the end.

I recently read an article about the Leader Dogs for the Blind executive training program near Detroit. No, the executives were not blind but being blindfolded and working with a guide dog taught them valuable lessons about managing people. One executive stated the tighter they pulled on the harness the less the dog was able to lead them. The executive went on to say that the harder you pull on your team the less they can help you achieve. The skills learned in this class included clear communication, team empowerment and trust in your team.

Part of not micromanaging your team is to give them enough information, so they can make their own decisions. A key is to treat you team like adults. I have seen micromanagers treat their team like teenagers and guess how they acted? You guessed it.

Part of not micromanaging is allowing your people to make mistakes. I heard a story of a new salesperson that made mistakes on an upcoming deal and lost the company over three million dollars. He was called into his boss's office and before the boss could say anything he said. "I'm sorry for messing up and I know you are going to fire me". The boss looked at him and said, "Are you kidding me? I just spend three million dollars training you, I'm not going to fire you now."

Use mistakes as learning tools and not excuses to fire employees that you didn't train properly in the first place.

3. **Express interest in your team member's success and well-being**. This starts on day one by making new team members feel welcome.

On the first day of class I always greet each student at the door with a smile and handshake introducing myself and welcoming them. This sets the tone for the semester. In business you need to make sure you are ready to onboard new employees by having a written training plan and schedule. I would share the schedule with new employees and walk them to and from each onboarding meeting or training giving them plenty of time to process what they were learning. You only have one opportunity to make a good first impression. This employee may work with you for the next several years, so it is worth the effort.

I always get to know my students and employees. I used the following interview sheet to conduct an introductory interview with each student and I followed it up with an exit interview at the end of class. The introductory interview was a great way to get to know the students, their strengths and what they were hoping to learn. The feedback was very positive and none of the students had ever had a one-on-one introductory interview with a professor before (unless they took my wife's business classes as I took the idea from her). Getting to know my students allowed me to tailor much of my teaching and provided better outcomes for the students. Just as in business it isn't about me it's about the students.

Student interview begin semester
BUS 2530 Semester _____

Name	
Current job title (if not working full or part time student)	
What is your major?	
How long have you been attending OCC?	

What do you hope to learn from this class?	
How many classes are you taking? What are they?	
What is the most exciting thing about Sales for you?	
Have you ever worked in Sales before?	

Student Exit Interview MKT 1020 Semester _____

Name	
Current job title	
Networking events you plan to attend in next few months?	
Will you join a trade association? If so, which one?	
What is your major?	

Has this course impacted your career? How?	
When will you graduate or transfer (to where)? Do you know how to apply for graduation?	
Have you made your schedule for next semester? Do you need help with it?	
What grade did you want in this class? Are you going to achieve it? If yes, what did you do to accomplish it? If	

not, what should you have done?	
Is there anything I can help you with related to school or career?	

I always get to know my employees and their interests and backgrounds. People are very interesting and unique, and I was always amazed at how intelligent and talented the people that I have worked with are. I always remember my employee's birthdays and special occasions. I have been lucky enough to have visited the homes of many of my employees meeting their spouses, siblings, kids and parents. This gave me a unique perspective on my employees that allowed me to contribute to their success.

4. **Be productive and results oriented**. One of my main goals as a sales manager was to solve the problems of my sales team. One of the

problems most sales people complained about was the amount of administrative work they had to do. I made it my mission to remove as many administrative tasks as I could to give my team more time to sell. I have seen many poor managers do just the opposite. They requested detailed reports on everything that was happening, would be happening and might be happening. Did this result in additional sales because the manager now had more information? Sadly, no, the only thing this did was give the manager information to explain to his boss why the team was not hitting their sales targets. The manager just wanted to appear like he knew what was going on when questioned by his boss.

The best thing a leader can do is properly train your people, give them the tools to succeed, empower them to make decisions and get out of their way. If my team members do not hit their goals, then the team will not hit their goals.

One of the best ways to be productive is to prioritize work. In their book *The One Thing*, authors Gary Keller and Jay Papasan ask the question "What's the ONE Thing you can do this week such that by doing it everything else would be easier or unnecessary?"

[22]   When you look at your to do list every morning it can be overwhelming some days. Looking closer there is ONE thing on the list that is the most important. ONE thing that completed would make the other items on the list much easier to achieve or so unimportant you could take them off the list. The authors go on to point out that once you decide on the ONE thing you will get accomplished you need to block some time to be assured it gets done. "Time blocking works on the premise that a calendar records appointments but doesn't care who those appointments are with. So, when you know your ONE Thing, make an appointment with yourself to tackle it. Every day great salespeople generate leads, great programmers program, and great artists paint. Take any profession or any position and fill in the blank. Great success shows up when time is devoted every day to becoming great." [22]

Another thing that robs you of results and productivity is multitasking. Professor Clifford Nass who completed a study of multi-taskers in 2009 says, "Multitaskers were just lousy at everything."

Multitasking is a lie.

It's a lie because nearly everyone accepts it as an effective thing to do. It's become so mainstream that people actually think it's something they should do, and do as often as possible. We not only hear talk about doing it, we even hear talk about getting better at it." "With research overwhelmingly clear, it seems insane that – knowing how multitasking leads to mistakes, poor choices, and stress – we attempt it anyway. Maybe it's just too tempting." [22]

5. **Be a good communicator and listen to your team.** One measure of a good leader is not how they handle good new but how they handle bad news from their team. "An outstanding manager gets the bad news first. Nobody wants to be the bearer of bad tidings, because that triggers the kill-the-messenger syndrome. If you're in charge, you have to encourage the flow of bad news, because if you don't, bad situations get worse – before you can stop the hemorrhaging." [20] If you overreact to hearing bad news, then be prepared to be kept in the dark and get blindsided by bad news down the road. General Colin Powell said, "Leadership is solving problems. The day soldiers stop bringing you their problems is the day you have stopped leading them. They have either lost confidence that you can help or concluded you do not care."

Generals are great examples of people who make tough decisions, under pressure when lives are at stake. I often have told my sales teams that "we are not brain surgeons or generals, if we make a mistake no one is going to die, so let's relax and make the best decision we can and move forward."

Being a good communicator is more about listening than talking. Remember it's not about you it's about your team. A good communicator encourages discussion and open dialogue. Listen to what your team has to say and address any concerns or issues that your team is having. Share information with your team about your industry and company. A good communicator shares the good news and the bad. I have had instances where I found out bad news about my company from a customer vs. hearing from my manager. Don't put your team in that position.

A good communicator knows that you must clearly communicate with your team and with others within and outside your organization. A lot can get lost in translation as marketing talks to engineering and sales talks to product development.

An activity that I use with my classes to emphasize the importance of clear communication, I call 'Picture This'. I split the class into teams of 4, one team member at one end of the room, two in the middle and one at the opposite end of the room. I give one team member, seated at one end of the room, a picture. A team member seated at the opposite end has a blank piece of paper. Of the two team members in the middle one can talk to the person with the picture and one can talk to the person with the blank sheet of paper who is tasked with reproducing the picture. The catch is that the team member with the picture cannot show it to the team member that they talk to. The team member with the picture can only describe it in geometric terms, i.e. if it is a house they cannot say roof, door, window, etc.... They also cannot use hand movements to describe the picture. The team member that talks to the person with the picture asks them about the picture and then meets the team member who talks to the drawer in the middle of the room. The information from the team member with the picture is then relayed to the person who is drawing the picture. Everyone is instructed to talk in a low enough tone that only the team member they are talking to can hear them. This is a challenging exercise and I give the teams about 10-15 minutes to complete.

Here is the picture.

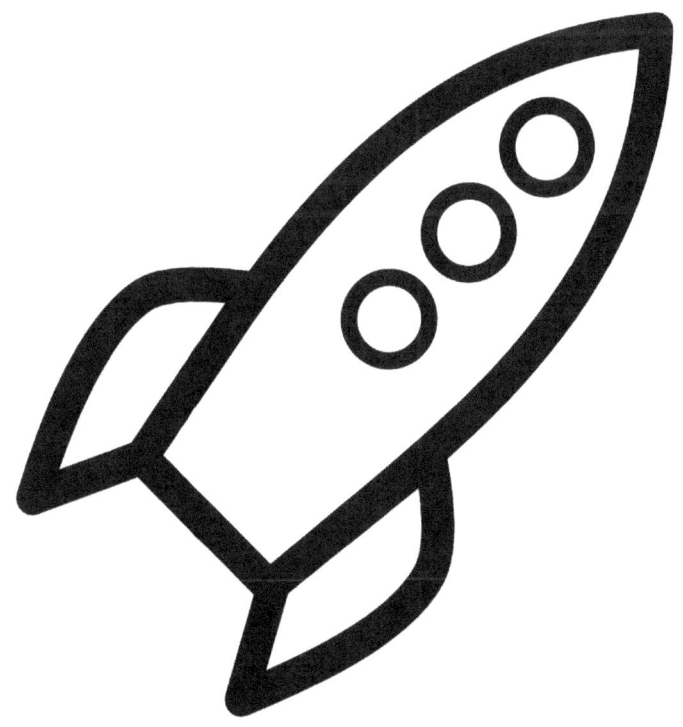

Here are some of the reproductions;

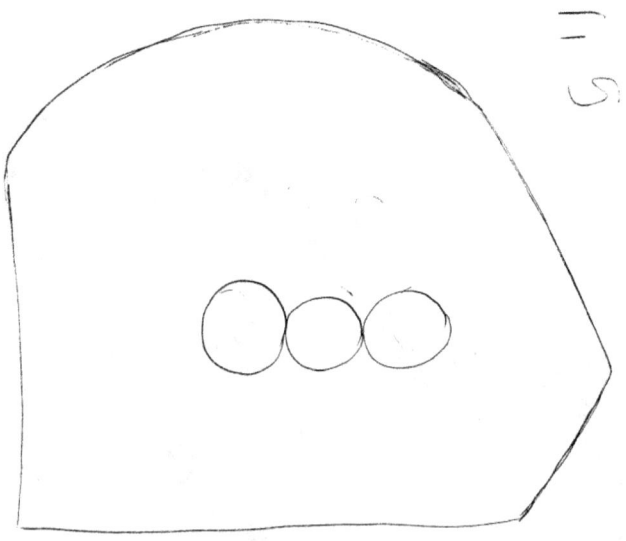

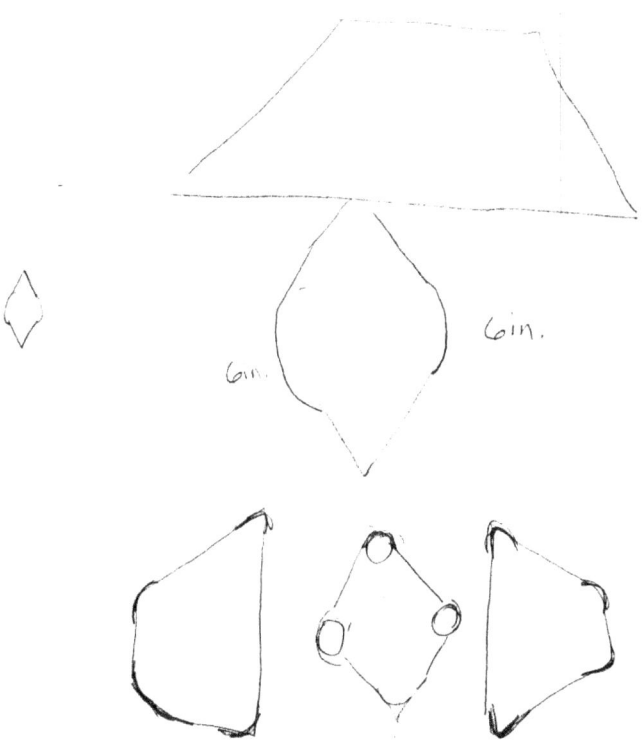

The reproductions usually have some characteristics of the original, but most team's reproductions are not recognizable as the original rocket. The activity really brings home how important it is to communicate for understanding. A leader makes sure their team understands what they are communicating. One person's rocket ship is another person's rounded rectangle or triangle with three circles in it.

6. **Help your employees with career development**. When I worked in the car rental industry I helped over two dozen people that I hired and trained reach the level of District Manager and beyond. I saw first-hand how motivated employees were when they knew that their hard work would lead to gains in income and career advancement. One thing a leader needs to do is find out what their team member's career aspirations are. Many employees want a promotion, but some may want to continue in the same job or after gaining experience move into another part of the company. You won't know until you ask. On the flip side if you do not help your employees with career advancement it will lead to low morale and high turnover. To help managers cut down on turnover and increase employee morale Google performs quarterly employee reviews vs. annual reviews. This led to a huge swing in positive ratings that employees gave their managers.

One of the most important things a leader can do is give sincere thanks to employees that do a good job and recognize their efforts. I worked for a company that added the core value of 'celebrating success'. I remember the first sales meeting after this core value was added. At the end of the meeting the VP of sales says, "I almost forgot to thank everyone and say congratulations for hitting our sales targets in the first quarter", now let's get ready for Q2 as our sales targets are increasing. Not much of a celebration and one the VP almost forgot. Celebrating success is not something that many sales managers are used to doing. I had a sales manager that once said, "my employees reward is that they still have jobs".

7. **Have a clear vision and strategy for the team.** One of the most important parts of creating a vision and strategy is including your customers and employees. What's that you say? Include your customers and your employees in vision and strategy, isn't that managements job? If you 'give' your sales team or customer a vision or strategy, then it isn't theirs, it's yours. If you include your employees and customers in the creating of a vision and strategy, then it is our vision and strategy. I always included my sales team and customers in the creation of vision, strategy and sales goals and I often found that their goals were higher than the ones that I had calculated, and we were much more likely to achieve our vision, strategy and hit the sales

goals after buy in from customers and employees.

One of the first steps in building a strategy is to know what you do well and what your competition does well. In their book *Blue Ocean Strategy,* authors W. Chan Kim and Rene'e Mauborgne, discuss the Strategy Canvas. "The strategy canvas is both a diagnostic and action framework for building a compelling blue ocean strategy. It serves two purposes. First, it captures the current state of play in the known market space. This allows you to understand where the competition is in products, service and delivery, and what customers receive from the existing competitive offerings on the market." [25] Second, the other axis allows you to see to what extend each company rates in these products and services. An example used in the book looked at the Strategy Canvas for Southwest Airlines, which compared the average airline, Southwest Airlines and car transportation. Car transport was included as an alternative industry.

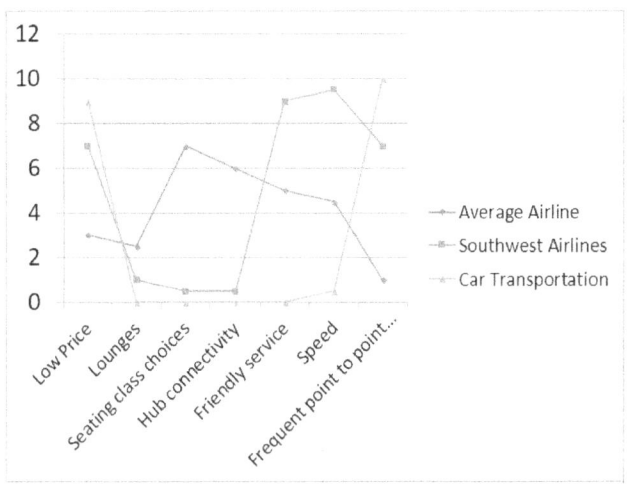

"Southwest Airline's created a blue ocean by breaking the trade-offs customers had to make between the speed of airplanes and the economy and flexibility of car transport. To achieve this, Southwest offered high-speed transport with frequent and flexible departures at prices attractive to the mass of buyers. By eliminating and reducing certain factors of competition and raising others in the traditional airline industry, as well as by creating new factors drawn from the alternative industry of car transport, Southwest Airlines was able to offer unprecedented utility for air travelers and achieve a leap in value with a low-cost business model."[25]   After you have graphed your strategy canvas it becomes clearer where you create value for the customer, where your focus should be and what you can reduce or eliminate.

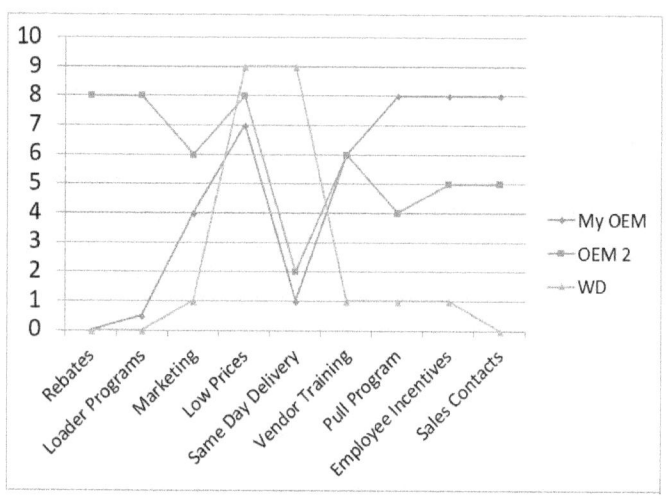

I created a strategy canvas for an OE truck manufacturer that I work for, concentrating on parts sales. I compared our company, a major competitor and a competitor in a related industry, an independent warehouse distributor. We did not offer rebates or loader programs or discounts to get customers to buy ahead. We did a pretty good job in marketing but not as good as our competitors. We did not have the lowest price. Same day delivery was not our strong suit. We provided vendor training and so did our competitors. We excelled in three areas;

Pull programs; Retail programs to help our dealers sell parts to their customers.

Employee incentives; We offered a once in a lifetime type trip to our dealers every year for hitting certain targets.   Destinations included Ireland, Monaco and Costa Rica.

We had the most professional sales team, which was also highly trained and motivated. Our biggest advantage was our salespeople.

We created value for our customers by helping them develop retail programs to sell the products they purchased from us. We continued to focus on training and motivating our employees and we did not offer rebates, loader programs or lowest prices.   We learned what our competitors did well, what we did well and concentrated on differentiating ourselves from our competitors. I had a sales trainer once say, "Find out what your competition is doing and don't do it. If they are big, go small. If they are cheap, be expensive." Differentiation is the key.

8. **Have technical skills so you can advise the team.**   A technology company like Google thought this would be one of the most important behaviors of a good boss, but it was last on the list. Turns out that employees want someone who has the other seven behaviors more than someone who has more technical expertise. This comes as no surprise to true

leaders because they know it's not about them it's about their employees. Leaders make sure they continually improve, and technical knowledge is a part of that. When I worked at GM I took a week-long course entitled 'Pop the Hood'. The course gave us hands on experience with vehicle parts and systems. We learned how the various parts functioned and why quality parts were important for safety and long life. It is important for leaders to have the technical knowledge to advise their team, but the other 7 skills are more important to a leader.

In his book, *Good to Great*, Jim Collins and his team spent a combined 15,000 hours of research on what took a company from the transition of being Good to Great. This research included stock market returns, reading fifty years of articles about companies, reviewing company strategy, technology, leadership and interviewing executives. They analyzed acquisitions, executive compensation, corporate culture, leadership style, layoffs, management turnover and financial ratios. An important part of their research was what made a great leader, termed Level Five Leadership. The level five executive "Builds enduring greatness through a paradoxical blend of personal humility and professional will." [26]

"The term Level 5 refers to the highest level in a hierarchy of executive capabilities that we defined in our research. Level 5 leaders channel their ego needs away from themselves and into the larger goal of building a great company. It's not that Level 5 leaders have no ego or self-interest. Indeed, they are incredibly ambitious – *but their ambition is first and foremost for the institution, not themselves*."[26] Jim and his team found level five leaders shared the following characteristics;

Ambitious first and foremost for the company, not themselves.

Set up successors for even greater success in the next generation.

Modest and self-effacing.

Fanatically driven to produce sustained results.

Workmanlike diligence, more plow horse than show horse.

Contribute success to factors other than themselves, like luck.

Take responsibility when things go poorly.

The level five leader understands that it is not about them it is about the company, employees and customers.

Chapter 10

The Secret Formula for Sales Success

A sales trainer once gave me the secret formula for sales success.

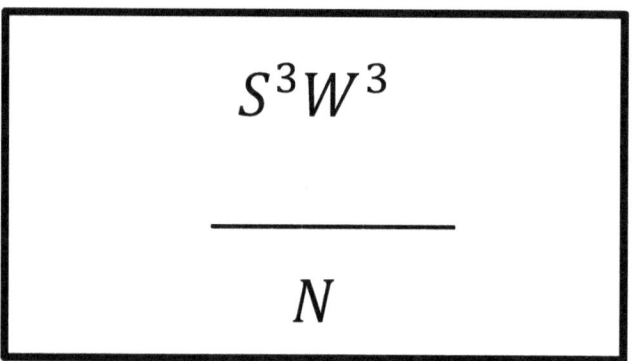

- *Some Will*
- *Some Won't*
- *So What*

- *Next!*

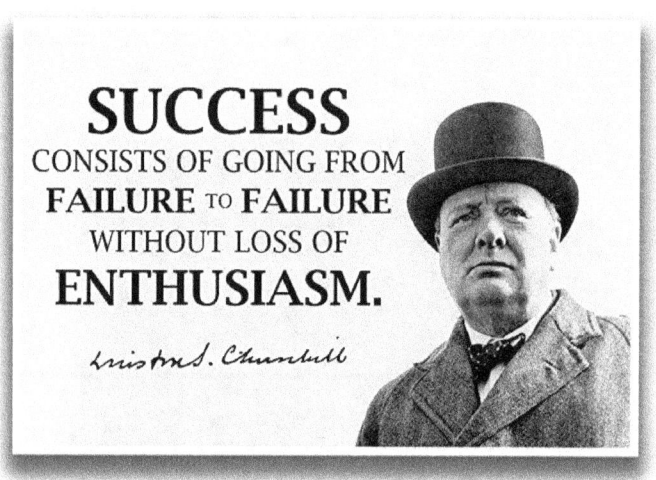

Remember that sales is not all or nothing and it helps to have a thick skin.

Good Selling!

Tom Hoffman and Cindy Hoffman

Chapter 11

Bringing it all Together

Chapter 1- Nothing Happens Until Somebody Sells Something

Everyone is a salesperson, kids are natural sales people.

Salespeople are the economic engine that runs our economy.

No matter what you do in life, selling is a part of it.

Chapter 2- The Salesperson Who Talks About Nothing but Price is a Loser

Don't be a loser.

It's not about the bike, it's about the culture.

Do my customers look forward to seeing me?

Chapter 3- What Successful Salespeople do

Listen.

Ask questions.

Solve problems.

Chapter 4- Preparing for and Executing Meetings and Presentations

It's hard to take notes with a fork in your hand.

What one thing do you want the audience to remember?

Be in the moment, it's not about you.

Chapter 5- Protect the Mother Lode

You can't take care of business until you first take care of yourself.

Create good habits.

It all works.

Chapter 6- Negotiating and Closing the Sale

Do your homework.

Win the race before it starts.

A 'NO' is pure gold.

Chapter 7- Lessons From Wile E. Coyote

Don't be afraid to ask for help.

Do a sales self-assessment.

Know your competitor's strengths and weaknesses.

Chapter 8- Mistakes Salespeople Make

Smile.

Sales is not all or nothing.

Answer your phone.

Chapter 9- Sales Leadership

Leadership is solving problems.

More plow horse than show horse.

Follow the leader, not the boss.

Chapter 10- Secret Formula for Sales Success

Next!

Use all the resources available to you. You are a sales professional making your living selling. Look for every opportunity to improve your sales skills and learn something new.   Invest in yourself. Use travel and windshield time. Look for opportunities to teach and coach others.

Be yourself, be honest, add value, solve the customers problems and LISTEN.

Good Selling.

Notes

1. Charles Duhigg (2012). *The Power of Habit.* Random House, NY. 25, 58, 77-78
2. Garr Reynolds (2012). *Presentation Zen.* New Riders, Berkeley, CA 94710.
3. Bob Arnot (1995). *Dr. Bob Arnot's Guide to Turning Back the Clock.* Little, Brown and Company (Canada) Limited, Canada, Toronto. 7
4. Dale Carnegie (1936). *How to Win Friends and Influence People.* Pocket Books a division of Simon and Schuster, Inc., New York, NY 10020. 43-44, 84-85, 92
5. David Mattson and Anthony Parinello (2009). *Five Minutes with VITO; Making the most of your selling time with the Very Important Top Officer.* Pegasus Media World, Beverly Hills, CA. 90212. 12, 51-52
6. Jeb Blount (2010). *People Buy You; The Real Secret to What Matters Most in Business.* John

Wiley and Sons, Hoboken, New Jersey. 58-59, 157, 192-193, 33, 29

7. Steven Power (2004). *Power Selling; Consult and Collaborate to Gain Competitive Distinction.* Power2Be Media, Ventura, CA. 66, 32

8. Matthew Dixon and Brent Adamson (2011). *The Challenger Sale; How to Take Control of the Customer Conversation.* Penguin, London, England. 41

9. *Quality Process Improvement Tools and Techniques* By Shoji Shiba and David Walden Massachusetts Institute of Technology and Center for Quality of Management, revision 6. 7/30/2002

10. John G. Miller (2004). QBQ, *The Question Behind the Question; What to Really Ask Yourself to Eliminate Blame, Complaining and Procrastination.* G.P. Putnam's Sons, NY. 18

11. *Medicine and Science in Sports and Medicine.* https://www.healthline.com/health/fitness-exercise/best-time-to-workout#2

12. Chris Voss and Tahl Raz (2016). *Never Split the Difference; Negotiating as if Your Life Depended On It.* Harper Collins, New York, NY. 10007. 16, 36, 50, 52, 65, 73, 75, 86, 91

13. John G. Miller (1998). *Personal Accountability; Powerful and Practical Ideas for You and Your*

Organization. Denver Press, Commerce City, CO 80022. 63

14. https://www.kidney.org/news/ekidney/march11/DoloresBisagni_March11

15. T. Scott Gross (1991). *Positively Outrageous Service; New and Easy Ways to Win Customers for Life.* Mastermedia Ltd., NY. 145, 154, 127

16. Ron Gutman. *The Hidden Power of Smiling.* TED talk, Ron Gutman

    (http://www.ted.com/talks/ron_gutman_the_hidden_power_of_smiling)

17. Mark H. McCormack (1984). *What They Don't Teach You at Harvard Business School.* Bantam Books, New York, NY.

18. http://www.cbsnews.com/news/inside-google-workplaces-from-perks-to-nap-pods/

19. http://www.nytimes.com/2011/03/13/business/13hire.html?_r=1&pagewanted=all

20. Harvey Mackay (1991). *Swim with the Sharks Without Being Eaten Alive; Outsell, Outmanage, Outmotivate and Outnegotiate Your Competition.* Ivy Books, New York, NY. 23, 130, 137

21. https://news.gallup.com/poll/241649/employee-engagement-rise.aspx

22. Gary Keller and Jay Papasan (2012). *The ONE Thing; The Surprisingly Simple Truth Behind Extraordinary Results.* Bard Press, Austin, TX. 9, 163, 44, 51

23. Simon Sinek (2009). *Start With Why; How Great Leaders Inspire Everyone to Take Action.* Penguin Group, New York, NY. 39, 45, 69

24. Jeffrey J. Fox (2015*). How to Become a Rainmaker; The Rules for Getting and Keeping Customers and Clients.* Hachette Books, New York, NY. 10104. 39

25. W. Chan Kim and Renee Mauborgne (2005). *Blue Ocean Strategy; How to Create Uncontested Market Space and Make the Competition Irrelevant.* Harvard Business School Publishing, Boston, MA. 25, 38

26. Jim Collins (2001). *Good to Great.* HarperCollins Books, New York, NY. 20, 21

27. https://www.smithsonianmag.com/science-nature/halitosis-horrors-how-bad-breath-became-americas-worst-nightmare-180962104/

28. Daniel Goleman (1994). *Emotional Intelligence; Why it can matter more than IQ.* Bantam Books, New York, NY.

29. Malcolm Gladwell (2008). *Outliers; The Story of Success.* Little, Brown and Company, New York, NY. 10017.

30. Chester L. Karrass (1996). *In Business As in Life – You Don't Get What You Deserve, You Get What You Negotiate.* Standford St. Press, Beverly Hills, CA. 90211. 393
31. Michael Michalko (2006). *Thinkertoys; A handbook of creative-thinking techniques.* Ten Speed Press, Berkeley, CA. 94707. 346-349

About the Authors

Thomas J. Hoffman, MBA has over 30 years of success in senior sales and sales leadership positions having made over 47,000 face-to-face sales calls. He is a business owner and has worked with several Fortune 100 companies including General Motors, FCA, Toyota, Navistar and Volvo/Mack. Hoffman is also an Adjunct Professor of business teaching sales and sales management and has an MBA from the University of Phoenix.

Cynthia D. Hoffman, Ph.D. is a serial entrepreneur. Her research and studies in Learning Design and Technology, specifically Human Performance Improvement, focus on the impact of in class mentoring activities on student perceptions. She is a currently a partner in Hoffman Business Consulting, LLC and full-time business faculty teaching marketing, management and entrepreneurship. She has a Ph.D. in Learning Design and Technology from Wayne State University.

Fresh Breath

is the Key to the

People Business

Lessons from

47,000

face-to-face sales calls

Thomas Hoffman MBA

Cynthia Hoffman PHD